C000245457

The Incredible V

Employee Power Unleashed

How to Gain Competitive
Advantage by Treating Your
Employees Well

By: Robertson Hunter Stewart

This book is dedicated to:

Bernard Granier

"A good man and a great boss"

ISBN: 9781076872159

The author of this work is:

Robertson Hunter Stewart
Born 1962 St. Andrews, Scotland

Table of Contents

Introduction
to
Employee Power

Introduction

Employee power is one of the biggest keys to success for any organisation. Today, people often speak about the importance of being guest or consumer centric and, of course, this is very true, particularly within the service sector.

Our current society, where communication is instantaneous and widespread and where the power of social media is no longer in question, gives an enormous amount of power to customers and potential customers. Bad reviews on social media can have disastrous consequences for a company's financial wellbeing and results, as we all know.

Today, it would seem to me that everyone knows and understands the above. However, in order to become (and stay) guest centric, your **employees** have to **believe** in what they are doing at all levels and be **motivated** to do it to the best of their ability. In short, in order to become guest centric, **you first have to be employee centric**.

This book is about **how to become and stay employee centric** and develop to the **maximum the employee power which already exists within your organisation.**

What is employee power?

A good question! My definition is as follows:

"The power produced by employees within an organisation which allows it to obtain and keep competitive advantage within the marketplace over time."

Why is it so important?

Quite simply, if you don't produce this power, someone else will and, to your disgust, you will find it will probably be your most direct competitor. Don't forget that in today's job market a company or organisation has to be attractive in order to have a chance of **getting the best talent on board** (more about talent management and recruitment later in the book).

How to produce employee power?

That is what this book is about: **read on!**

The first and most obvious thing to say is that in order to produce adequate **employee power,** the strategy of the company or organisation has to be heavily centred on what I would call the **employee experience.**

This, of course, starts very early on for any employee with their **recruitment experience,** followed very closely by their **integration experience** and then by their **experience whilst working** for the company. You can also easily see how this relates well to the guest experience or guest cycle for service sectors such as hotels and restaurants. In its simplest form, the employee experience cycle could be shown as follows:

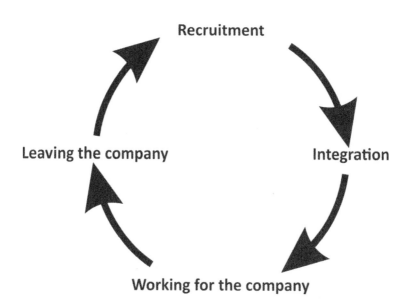

Recruitment

Integration

Working for the company

Leaving the company

At some stage, you will all have been through this cycle and understand what the various potential impacts on yourself as a person might be (or have been) at each of the various stages.

This book is therefore addressed to you and, more specifically, to all of the people who have been and are employees. Fundamentally, it is aimed at anyone who works with or manages others, no matter whether this is an intention at the moment (you are a management student), whether you are already a manager or whatever stage in your career you might have reached at this moment in time.

Subjects covered in the book include how to become employee centric (or more so). Other topics which will be talked about in depth include employee recognition, training, the importance of meetings and the complementary nature of the relationship between products and services. All of the aforementioned are inter-related to some degree or other and are each crucial to the success of any business in their own right. I believe that this has always been true but that it is even more so today, with a future where being employee centric will become hypercritical for all organisations.

Another area which will be a recurrent theme throughout this book is the importance of giving more autonomy to employees as a first step towards empowerment. This is a subject that has been on the "business agenda" for such a long time but far too often ignored. If not ignored, it is often put in place with a complete lack of gusto, enthusiasm or belief, in certain cases.

This will no longer be possible as it is no longer a "want it" or "nice to have" on the part of employees.

This is and will remain an absolute necessity in the workplace. It can still, of course, be ignored but I am suggesting that if companies take this route, it will be at their own risk and peril!

The way that employees interact with one another and how we interact with them on a daily basis truly will become **the defining factor** for all businesses that want and need to succeed from now on.

As with "consumer power", "employee power" is already here (and here to stay). It is becoming the key source of competitive advantage for companies both now and in the future.

Throughout this book, you will find that there are a large number of examples from the hotel industry. If you are not from this industry, please accept my apologies for this in advance. Nevertheless, everything written in this book applies to all forms and types of industry, whether they are primary, secondary or tertiary. This is quite simply because human beings and employees are always involved at some stage.

As to the main reasons I have written this book, they are clearly explained in the brief history which follows this introduction. However, the most fundamental reason is that I firmly believe that **employees** are **the most important** asset or **resource** for any company and that without employees who are happy, well-motivated and engaged with the company, simply put, **NOTHING WORKS!**

Chapter One

A Brief History

A Brief History

The first question that I asked myself before writing this book was why?

There are a number of reasons why I wrote this book and first among them is that I have been an employee for most of my professional life and have had good, bad and indifferent experiences throughout (which of course probably doesn't make me different from anyone else).

My experience as an employee has now stretched over a period of 36 years (I am 56-years-old at the time of writing) and the last 26 years have been spent in the service sector. In the course of this time, I have been very well treated, very badly treated and, of course, at some stages in my career, completely ignored.

As both an employee and a manager, I strongly believe that the **way that we are treated** within an organisation impacts to a very high degree on **how we behave** as employees and, following on from that, **how we perform**.

When I arrived in France in **1992,** I spoke absolutely no French (not even a smattering at school textbook level), apart from *"Jean Pierre a perdu le ballon dans le jardin"*.

I considered myself very lucky to get a job at Euro Disney (luckily they were on the lookout for English speakers at the time ☺). This was in Paris during the opening of the park and hotels in April 1992. Because I didn't speak any French at the time, I was offered **my first job as a cleaner** and, by the time I left, I was what is called a "Small World Manager" in charge of cleaning and costuming at the Disney Village.

I then went on to become the first male Executive Housekeeper for a large-scale hotel operation in Paris (over 1000 rooms) before becoming Operations Manager for luxury hotels in both Poland and Hungary. On returning to France, I was **General Manager** at one time or another for three of the **biggest hotels in Europe** (all with 1000 rooms or over).

Of course, I could go into a lot more detail regarding my own career but then that is **definitely not the point!**

SO WHAT IS THE POINT?

The point is that I have **been an employee** in some very large organisations together **with a lot of other employees** and this has been **at a number of different levels**:

- ➢ As an employee
- ➢ As a supervisor
- ➢ As a junior manager
- ➢ As a senior manager
- ➢ As a leader

But, still, at the end of the day, an employee and an employee willing to learn from my own mistakes and the mistakes of others (including those of organisations as a whole and those of other employees and managers).

And what is the most important thing that I have learned about employees?

Please see the next page

EMPLOYEES ARE FIRST AND FOREMOST HUMAN BEINGS SO DON'T FORGET IT!

So definitely no rocket science involved there, then!

However, I, for one, definitely believe that this simple fact is **all too often forgotten**. We tend to forget that the people that we are working with have lives outside of work and that the **life-work balance** that so many people talk about is not respected (this can be due to employees themselves, their colleagues or indeed their employer). A lot of the time, though, this can be due to the employer, **whether or not this is intentional!**

You've probably worked out by now another of the reasons I wrote this book?

If not, here it is:

I truly and sincerely believe, based on my own personal experience as an employee, that people should be treated well within organisations both from a humanistic point of view and for business reasons.

This book is about convincing anyone that might read it of the **fundamental value of employees** and about showing in a concrete manner what can be done to tap into the **incredible energy of employee power**.

The final reason I wrote this book is to do with inspiration from some great leaders!

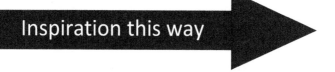

Inspiration this way

Some edifying quotes:

"Train people well enough so that they can leave, treat them well enough so that they don't."

Richard Branson

"Take good care of your employees, and they'll take good care of your customers, and the customers will come back."

JW Marriott

"Always treat your employees exactly as you want them to treat your best customers."

Stephen Covey

Chapter Two

Employees

Employees

So, if we believe that employees are to be treated well and are central to the success of any company or organisation, the very first thing we should be looking at is what exactly are the wants and needs of our primary resource!

Regarding the needs and wants of employees and based on what I have already said, as well as upon my own experience, the following sums it up quite nicely:

1. To be well treated;
2. To work in a good atmosphere;
3. To have the right tools to do one's job;
4. To be well paid.

The fourth point seems rather obvious and you may think that I am over-simplifying things here (Taylorism: "A fair day's work for a fair day's pay"). Nevertheless, although other criteria can be important to employees, I really do think that if the pay scales (or benefit packages, if you prefer) are not in line with the market where the company is operating, you will soon find it difficult to recruit and/or keep employees.

This is why it is so important for Human Resources in companies today to know what the "going rate" is for the various job functions within their organisations. You have probably all heard the following at one time or another: **"If you pay peanuts, you are going to get monkeys"**.

Although paying people correctly is extremely important, it is not one of the central themes of this book. The central themes are 1 to 3 from the previous page. If we look at these in the format of a diagram, it gives us the following:

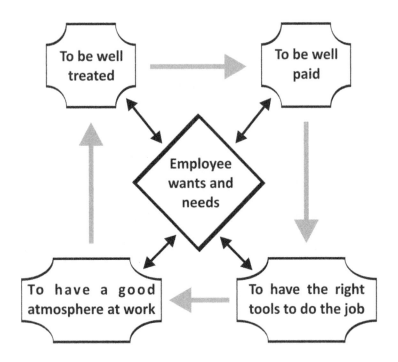

As I said earlier, to be well paid is not the central theme of this book, although it probably does merit a book on the subject wholly by itself. If we look further at the three subjects we will be looking at in more detail, we can see the following:

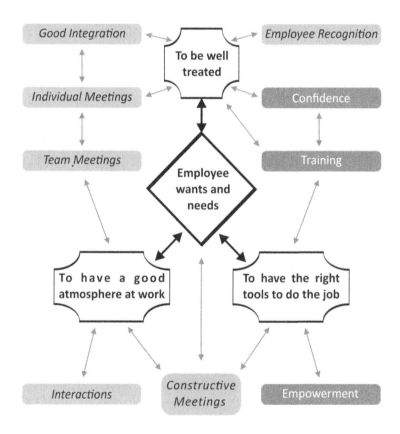

All of the areas on the previous page are within the scope of this book.

As you can see, everything in this diagram is pointing towards the centre: what the employee needs and wants. This has been done in order to further highlight that employees are not only central to the organisation, but that everything should be done to ensure that the needs and wants of your employees are met as they are central to the success of your organisation. However, do note the following:

YOU **MIGHT NOT** FULFILL YOUR EMPLOYEES' NEEDS ALL OF THE TIME, BUT YOU SHOULD **BE AIMING** TOWARDS THIS ALL OF THE TIME.

In other words, every effort should be made to ensure that your organisation is as **employee centric** as possible because this is the **real key to employee power!**

At this point, it's probably a good idea to think about what our own wants and needs have been in the past as well as in the present. In my own case as an employee, when I carry out some introspection around this subject, I tend to think about what I don't want first (just like a lot of other people, I suppose). Thinking further on this, there is very often one thing that "leaps" to the front. Any guesses? That's right: to work for a company or a person that gives me absolutely no autonomy at all to do my job "in the best way I see fit".

In my own experience, it does not matter at what level you are at for this to hold true, whether you are an extremely junior employee or more senior in your employee experience. To take the point further, if you have a cleaner who is excellent at his/her job and who always obtains "sparkling" results why would you micro-manage this person? You'd be much better off congratulating the person for their great work and results. Needless to say, this type of positive reinforcement can and usually will lead to better and better results (an upward spiral).

Now imagine that you have a senior manager who is meant to be running a department who is being "micro-managed" to the point that he/she is not allowed to order office supplies for his/her team and requires authorisation from his/her direct superior? Apart from the fact that I have personally seen this happen, do you think this is normal? Would you as an employee like to be in this situation yourself? Going further than that, do you think that your team will be impressed by this? Put another way, do you think that this will help make you legitimate in your role as a manager/leader? The answer to all of this is a very big and obvious no! Unfortunately, this still exists even for very senior managers within organisations today. Organisations that are acting in this way really are "shooting themselves in the foot", especially considering the speed at which things change with today's globalised technology and innovation-led environment.

A recent analysis from Gallup shows that, when organisations reach 1,000 or more employees in size, the percentage of people who believe that they have the opportunity to do best what they do every day and who have the feeling that their job is important for the company goes down. Added to this, Gallup statistics also tell us that in the United States, 51% of employees are either looking for a new job or on the lookout for new opportunities.

At the end of 2016 (a long time ago in today's terms), a study was carried out by one of the biggest labour unions in France with 200,000 participants. The result of this was that 75% of the employees spoken to indicated that they wanted to have more autonomy at work (the study was called "parlons travail" and was carried out in the fourth quarter of 2016). I think you would also find that if we looked at the employees who are entering the workplace today; this number is just getting bigger and bigger. I would underline here that this subject is becoming central to retaining employees, which on its own is one of the most major issues for companies today and will become even more so in the future.

Why do I say that? Well, because I have had many conversations with employees in various walks of life and different industries recently and one thing that they all agree on is that they are finding the lack of autonomy in the workplace more and more unbearable and, by the same token, unacceptable.

This can often be to the extent that it is one of the major reasons that they leave their jobs, as certain employees have been telling me recently! We will talk more about increasing employee autonomy later in the book and indeed how to maximise this and take it to new levels. This will definitely become one of the major strategic goals for companies and organisations both now and in the future.

Whilst we are on the subject of what employees don't want, in equal first place with having no autonomy at work comes working for a really bad boss! If we look at social media today, an awful lot is being written which talks about the "toxic boss" and just how much this type of boss can damage your most important asset (your employees). So, just what is a toxic boss?

Well I suppose the best clue is in the expression itself. This **is someone who has the same effect on the atmosphere at work that pollution has on the ozone layer of our planet's atmosphere.** That is to say, he/she destroys it.

This is, of course, already bad enough but it is only the beginning when you consider that this type of boss or manager can also dramatically affect the psychological wellbeing and health of the people who work with and for him. Going back to a point touched on earlier, these types of managers tend to micro-manage as well as abuse their "authority" and take credit for things which have actually been done by the employees who work with them (and who of course do not receive any credit or reward for their extra efforts or ideas).

Recent Gallup organisational research indicates that "Managers account for at least 70% of the variance in employee engagement scores". All of the evidence does seem to be pointing in the same direction telling us that employees need to be given autonomy and be motivated towards more engagement with the company or organisation.

Do remember, though, that your managers and bosses are also employees of the organisation and that perhaps they might have become as they are from being ill-treated themselves. Nevertheless, as a leader or future leader of an organisation or team, you must not allow this type of bullying to take place at work and sometimes you just have "to bite the bullet" and say goodbye to this type of individual for the greater good (and I for one would strongly suggest that you do).

You all know the story about leaving the rotten apple in the barrel: if you do, you are risking losing all of the apples and, in this case, we are talking about losing valuable employees who are expensive to replace and who might in certain cases prove to be irreplaceable.

I will grant that none of this sounds very positive but do remember that even if an employee "loves" the company he is working for, he will leave if his boss is toxic. This is because **people work first and foremost for other people and not for companies.**

On the subject of employees, do remember that, in spite of the importance of building teams and group cohesion, employees are first and foremost individuals and furthermore they are "like snowflakes!" What I mean here is that they are all different from one another and that they should not only be treated as members of a team but also as individuals. We will talk about this in several different areas of the book a bit later on.

Do also remember that there are different groups of employees in the workplace who are of different ages, sex and experience or social backgrounds, who come from differing horizons and cultures and who have different and varying levels of expertise. Although this is not a book about diversity (cultural or otherwise), I do believe that when you are in charge of an organisation you do have to understand that in today's global environment these differences should be embraced. To be more precise, I do firmly believe that teams which are heterogeneous can be and often are more valuable than teams which are extremely homogeneous.

If you think about it, if you put a whole load of employees together who are extremely "like minded" for any decent length of time, they are very likely to end up agreeing with one another on a very wide variety of subjects and very probably most, if not all of the time. If, on the other hand, you do the same exercise with people who are very different from one another, although there may be some "minor conflicts" to sort out, you are very probably going to create a more fertile environment in terms of creativity.

One area which is often ignored in organisations with regard to employees is what I like to call the importance of an inter-generational approach. Put simply, don't forget your seniors! Experience from seniors counts just as much as the enthusiasm of your younger employees and sometimes, believe it or not, **even more so**. Don't get me wrong here, enthusiasm is a great thing but **because someone is older does not necessarily mean that they are less enthusiastic or less creative than someone younger!**

As a case in point, a lot of organisations have quite recently put in place what they like to call a Shadow Executive Committee. This is on the face of it a great idea and helps to create value for the company by allowing juniors to give a different perspective with regards to the future strategy of the company by comparing their ideas and decisions with the actual Executive Committee. As I said, great idea! So what could possibly go wrong with that?

Well, in some cases, the creation of these shadow committees has had a tendency to use only junior employees. This in effect is limiting for several reasons not least of which is due to the frustration of some more senior (and, yes, older) employees who might and do find this rather insulting.

Not only that, but what if it is an older employee who is going to have the idea which could be a huge game changer for the company! More senior employees can also be very helpful with regards to mentoring and coaching their younger counterparts and I will talk a bit more about this later on.

Also, do remember from this example that I am not saying that older employees are better. What I am saying is that balance is required and that diversity can be a real key to success and can help with the creation of a base from which to work on the **creation of value** for the company or what I am calling **employee power.**

Do also remember that throughout this book the main paradigm **is** about being employee centric or, as Richard Branson put it:

"Clients do not come first, employees come first. If you take care of your employees, they will take care of your clients."

Let's now start looking at how we are going to become a **more employee-powered and employee-centric organisation.**

Chapter Three

Being Employee Centric

Being Employee Centric

In Chapter One, I spoke about what motivated me to write this book. Motivation is indeed both a critical and central concept of the book itself. Overall, what we are talking about here is how to motivate your employees so that we can **use the combined power of these people to improve the performance of the organisation** (I should say that from here onwards I will use the term organisation interchangeably with company and/or both.)

The very first thing you need to do is to convince the people who run the company that **employee power** is a must for the competitive positioning of your company and that it is **fundamental as a strategic objective** for the organisation as a whole!

You might ask yourself: How exactly am I going to convince people?

Some answers to this might be:

- ➢ **Use the quotes from the previous chapter.**
- ➢ **Ask quite simply how employees would like to be treated?**
- ➢ **Brainstorm with employees why they are important for the company.**
- ➢ **Organise your next seminar on the subject of employee satisfaction and loyalty, and their importance.**

First and foremost, you have to be convinced yourself that this is the way forward for the organisation and you should plan carefully just how you are going to convince the other decision makers in the company (that is, if it's not you).

Going back to the earlier ideas, I would strongly suggest that you carry out a brainstorming session with both your senior and middle management around the subject of employee power so as to ensure that these two levels of employees are completely engaged with the importance of the organisation becoming employee centric. Why is this a good idea? Well, if you are preaching the importance of this, you have to remember that your executives and middle management are also employees and that, if you are going to be talking about the importance of this subject, you really need to do everything in your power so as to ensure that these employees collaborate in a very active way with their input and indeed with putting in place and actively supporting this strategy.

If you don't do this, you are quite simply "not practicing what you preach" and, in terms of leading by example, this would be truly awful. On the other hand, if you introduce this subject to your closest collaborators and they help you to produce and put in place the strategy, they are going to be very motivated to ensure that it works!

Once everyone is convinced and your executive team is all geared up and ready to go, the next thing you need to do is to look at how employee centric you are at the current time. One very good place to start is to see whether or not you are, in any way, shape or form, measuring **employee satisfaction?**

As someone famous once said:

"If you can't measure it you can't manage it."
Peter Drucker

So, if you don't have this measure in place in your organisation, I would strongly recommend that you do this **ASAP.** In any case, if you really are looking towards improving on it, there is no choice but to measure employee satisfaction or engagement. As said earlier, there really is no choice in the current business environment. Getting the design of a satisfaction survey right is crucial for two fundamental reasons.

First, it should not only be able to give you measureable criteria that can give an insight into how your employees are feeling at a certain point in time and what the priorities are in terms of their wants and needs. It should also give you actionable criteria which can be used as the basis for action plans for further improvement.

One piece of advice here: take your time getting this right. Although there are ways of **doing this in house** and for free (using, for example, Survey Monkey), you definitely would be better to get a **professional organisation** involved to **design an employee satisfaction survey.**

Before getting the professionals involved, though, you really need to ensure that the criteria that are being measured by the employee satisfaction survey are the right ones (what I mean by this is that the measures are relevant) and that you have appropriate tools in place to allow you to interpret and, indeed, use these results correctly. Here, again, you should be looking at the questions to be asked with your closest team members. Don't on any account exclude them from this exercise as you really do need to get this right.

The best idea could be to get the professionals involved to give you advice once you and your team have a good idea on where you want to take this and once you have in have mind the principal objectives as to why you need this information and what you are going to be using it for.

If you already have a customer satisfaction survey in place or are monitoring in some way your guest or consumer comments (and I sincerely hope that you are), this can provide a good frame of reference for the future design of your employee satisfaction survey. After all, in your drive towards becoming more and more employee centric, you should be treating your employees as your internal customers! As you can see, a lot of planning and thought should go into this exercise.

But don't waste time!

YOU NEED TO GET THE SHOW ON THE ROAD WITHOUT WAITING FOR THE RESULTS OF YOUR FIRST EMPLOYEE SATISFACTION AUDIT!

Communicate with your employees as **from now**. For example, let them know that you are putting in place the Employee Satisfaction Survey and how important this is for their future and, indeed, for the future of the company.

Once you have the results of the satisfaction survey, whether you have just put this in place or this is the last in a long series of surveys (a bit of friendly irony here), you need to take the results seriously and you really need to take the time to both analyse these results and look at how you can **best interpret** them. I really must insist here as, in my experience, as well as the numerous experiences that people have been kind enough to share with me, this has not been given nearly enough importance either in the past or today, as yet.

On the other hand, people have been telling me that an enormous amount of time and energy is spent ensuring that all of the data concerning guest feedback and strategies concerning guest-centric action plans are given priority over ensuring that the employees in the organisation are happy.

This is a dreadful mistake!

Yes, I know that this might sound a bit too much, but I for one don't believe that this is the case. The most important thing that must come first are your employees and not your guests or your clients. I am not the only one that thinks like this (see the earlier quote from Richard Branson).

You should be spending just as much time (if not more) analysing your employee satisfaction results and putting in place action plans to improve them. In any case, we all know that the people who have the vast majority of contact with our clients are our operational employees.

Good old common sense would tell you "Happy employee = Happy customer"! I do know that this phrase has been "on the go" and "bandied about" for a heck of a long time now.

One could even go so far as saying: why bother stating the obvious? My answer here would be because **too few organisations are actually doing something about it**.

At the very least, this would mean doing absolutely everything possible so as to ensure that your employees are happy in their place of work. If they are not smiling at and being nice to your customers, your customer reviews are not going to be great and this I can guarantee!

Being employee centric is also about your "mind set". What I mean by this is how you think about employees and how often you think about them. Let's take the second one first: how often we think about employees.

In my own case, when in charge of or working with teams, however big or small, I have tended to be "eating, drinking and sleeping" the team and nearly to the point of obsession! Constantly thinking about ways to improve my own communication with the team or individual team members, for example. Also thinking about conversations I have had with people during the day, writing down ideas that fellow employees have been good enough to share with me. Thinking about whether or not I used the right words in that appraisal interview I had with one of my managers today.

Going even further: How can I improve my own interpersonal communication skills so as to ensure that I am properly understood and that I can find the right words to motivate individuals or teams. Asking myself questions such as "was I fair in everything that I said to and did with my team today?"

And what about how I tend to think about employees? Well, for a start, in a very positive way, in the sense that I believe that the vast majority of employees are good employees or have the potential to be. This does not mean that I am in any way naive; we all know that there are a few "black sheep" out there. It does mean, though, that I have a very strong tendency to believe in people's ability to be good at things, to learn and to improve.

To sum up, being employee centric is about caring for your employees and creating the environment and work space within which they can flourish. Giving adequate care and attention to your employees is for me the same thing as investing in the company's future.

You have to start to recognise the value of your employees and **start letting them know.** The next chapter talks about how to go about this in some detail. Read on!

Chapter Four

Employee Recognition

Employee Recognition

LISTENING TO EMPLOYEES

On the previous page, we started talking about recognising the value of your employees and doing it NOW.

As employee recognition is a potentially vast subject, the question might be: where should I start with all of this?

My suggestion, here, is to start at the beginning by showing interest in your employees and listening to them and not just relying on an employee satisfaction survey which you might carry out once a year (although, of course, the feedback from this will be invaluable, as I have already said).

For me, a really good place to start is with the following mnemonic:

Employees

Are

Really

Everything

So, if employees really are the most important resource for the organisation, it really is important to listen to them. In order to better understand this, we will first look at the why and then the how.

As to why, let's start by having a look at the following mind map:

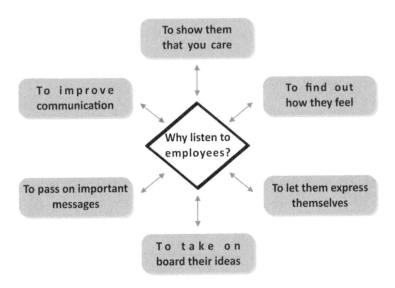

SHOW THEM THAT YOU CARE

Customers

Are

Really

Everything

Remember that first and foremost your **employees are your internal customers**. For this reason alone, you do not have a choice: you must listen to your employees. Of course, this does not mean that they are always right. Indeed, discretion must be used so as not be submerged when listening to these customers.

The very act itself of listening to your employees will start to give them some idea of their own importance and their **importance to the organisation.**

After all, **if you decide to ignore your customers** in today's market or not to act on what they are telling you, your organisation is not likely to be highly successful. It is exactly the same for your employees. Yes, you can choose to ignore them or not listen to them.

However, if you do choose to **ignore/not listen to employees,** several different things might happen such as their **leaving the organisation**. You might say that in certain cases this could be a good thing, which may be true in the case of certain employees, However, it will certainly also be true for **good employees** who will, after all, be **more at ease and have more opportunity to leave the organisation** in most instances.

Do also remember that, if you lose employees who offer potential to the competition, there are at least three negative effects:

1. It will cost you time and money to replace them and to train their replacements.
2. It will cost you in terms of your reputation as a good employer.
3. Good employees going to the competition will also cost you money because you will be offering them a source of competitive advantage.

If you want employees to stay and become fans of your organisation, you really do need to listen and not just pretend to be listening for the "sake of form". You have to listen both actively and attentively so that the employees you are interacting with realise that not only are you giving your time to them but also that **you do actually care about what they are saying!**

FIND OUT HOW THEY FEEL

I could have called this passage in the book taking the temperature!

What I'm talking about here is taking the "social temperature" of the company. Yes, you might always have some employees that don't feel good about working with you or the organisation but, if it is the vast majority, your company is in trouble!

Of course, there are some very obvious ways for employees to tell you that they are not well at or in the workplace, such as a strike or a go slow.

Without talking about this scenario, you might have certain segments within the workforce that have more problems than others.

For example, perhaps all the blue collar workers seem to be quite happy, whilst the others are unhappy. In another instance, it might be that the whole management population is unhappy and the opposite on the "shop floor".

The most important thing that you have to look for "**when taking the temperature**" like a good doctor would do is to **accurately measure the temperature** and then find out the root cause of the "illness". In other words, the why of employees' feeling the way they do.

This is always equally important whether the employee is feeling good, bad or indifferent!

Employees who feel good

These employees are a great place to start with when you want to start building employee power. What is really important is to **find out exactly why they are feeling good** and then **build on this**.

There might be an enormous number of reasons why one particular employee feels good and this reason may or may not be useful for the organisation as a whole (as the reason might not be work related, for example). If, however, you discover that there are a **large number of employees** who are **happy for the same reasons** and that these reasons are **work related,** then you really have something on which to build.

If you found out, for example, that a very large number of employees were very happy that an employee satisfaction survey was going to be put in place, then you should make sure to act on this and get the survey in place **ASAP**.

Employees who feel bad

These employees could be feeling bad or uncomfortable at their place of work for a very large number of reasons (including those of a personal nature). Perhaps they have a bad manager, don't get along well with their colleagues or don't have the right equipment to work with!

The list here could be very long but **sometimes the solution might be very simple** indeed. As a case in point, let me give you an example. In a large hotel structure, imagine that you have got very low satisfaction scores from the room maids' employee satisfaction survey scores.

If you dug into this to find out exactly why this was happening, you might be **extremely surprised by some of the results** (and you'll see why on the next page).

Although the reasons might be multiple, some of them might also be easy to understand (and easy to fix):

> There were not enough vacuum cleaners for all of the maids (they had to share and this held them up in their work).
> The supervisors were sending them back to re-clean rooms which had been checked for reasons such as "the toilet paper was not folded properly" instead of doing this themselves and asking the room maid to pay more attention to this in the future.
> The fact that they were cleaning the rooms together with another maid and were then being blamed as a team when the room had a problem related to cleanliness (perhaps more individual responsibility and autonomy if the maids were cleaning rooms individually?)
> The fact that they were not allowed their personal telephone on their person whilst working in the hotel rooms.

Even without being from the hotel or service sector, I think you can see that the solutions to all of these are self-evident. Indeed, these could all be solved very easily and lead to **happier, more productive and more quality-orientated employees.** This, of course, leads to the conclusion that we should never forget **common sense when dealing with other people.**

However, let's take a look at the example of not being allowed personal telephones whilst working in the hotel rooms. When you ask **Housekeeping Management** why this was the case, the general answer might very well be the following:

"Because we **can't have any confidence in the maids** and **we know** that they are going to spend time **on their phones** and most likely **in front of the guest!**"

What questions would you then ask the Housekeeping Management? I would suggest the following:

> ➢ Are you as a housekeeping manager allowed to have your personal telephone with you when you are on the guest floors in the hotel?
> ➢ If the answer to the above is yes, you could then ask them if they think this is fair?
> ➢ What happens if the room maid has an urgent personal call regarding a problem at school or when one of their children is sick?
> ➢ Does the housekeeping manager think that the fact that it is forbidden to use the telephone is really going to stop them doing it in this day and age?

I think you've got the idea, which is to **be fair** in what you do. Fairness is one of the most fundamental core values when you are building **relationships** with your employees **based on mutual trust**.

Employees who feel fine (indifferent)

These employees are "fine"; they come to work, they work and then they go home.

BUT

What if you could make them feel good about what they are doing or even great!

For these employees, common sense would tell you that they could become employees who feel bad or, on the contrary, great. Just because they are fine does not mean that you have to stop recognising them. On the contrary, reinforce the recognition that you are giving them. The quote on the next page is very refreshing in this sense (and also applies very much to employees who feel good):

To be honest I found this quote on LinkedIn, so judge for yourself whether you agree or not.

"Do not give him a big pay rise, he is loyal. He is not going anywhere."

Some bosses think this way.

"Rewarding loyalty by paying less is dumb. If you push loyal people hard enough, they will quit. Loyalty should be rewarded not punished!"

I believe that the above sums things up quite well with regards to how people might feel within an organisation. Remember **whether or not employees feel good, bad or indifferent within organisations, they all represent golden opportunities in terms of building employee power.**

Let's now move on to the next of the whys, namely:

To let employees express themselves.

LET THEM EXPRESS THEMSELVES

I think we would agree in saying that it would not be very useful to show employees that you care, try and find out how they feel and **then not listen to them.**

What I am talking about here is to take care when you are meeting with employees so as to ensure that they have adequate opportunities to talk and that you don't interrupt when they are talking. Listen to them attentively. One good way of ensuring this is to take notes whilst they are talking.

As we said earlier, the very act of listening to your employees attentively shows that you care about what they have to say and this is an **important first step on the way to creating employee power!**

However, giving employees the opportunity to talk and be listened to (and not just heard) is not the only way or form of expression which is important.

We could also talk about . . .

EMPOWERMENT

YES, you've guessed it!!

EMPOWERMENT

Over the years, a lot has been said and written about this subject. It may seem obvious, but what it really means is to **give employees the power to do their job!**

This means allowing them to be creative and, indeed, even to take risks and, **god forbid, decisions!**

So many managers *talk and talk and talk* about empowering their employees to make decisions on the "shop floor" and the first thing that happens when an employee makes a **mistake** or takes the wrong decision is that the manager arrives to scream at them and in some cases even go as far putting in place **disciplinary action.**

Striking fear into the hearts of your employees is definitely not the way to go.

On the contrary, you should **congratulate them for having taken a decision** even if it is the wrong one and take the time to explain how they can **improve on this the next time.**

Of course, there are limits to this and it does depend on the consequences of the decision made and whether or not the employee in question has made the same mistake 100 times already!

VERY IMPORTANT

Do not forget to congratulate and recognise employees who are getting decisions right all the time. This is called **positive reinforcement** and leads to the sharing and, indeed, **spreading of good behaviours amongst your employees**.

Empowerment is also to do with confidence and trust. If you think about the concepts of confidence and trust in your life outside of work, I am sure that most of you would agree that, if there is no trust within, for example, a family unit, there is a great likelihood that this will lead to a serious problem at some stage and quite likely the ending or breaking of one or more relationships. Obviously, not a healthy situation.

I believe that this also applies to organisations and companies and that you should do everything possible to give your trust to your employees and show them that you are confident in their abilities. In order to achieve this, I am a great fan of taking empowerment as far as it can possibly go both for the reasons that I have just given but also for another equally important reason.

The reason is that if employees on the shop floor are not able to make decisions in real-time situations with the guest or customer in front of them, this puts both the employee and the customer in a very awkward position.

This is not only extremely embarrassing for the employee who finds himself in this situation but is also not at all guest centric. Think of yourself as the guest. Who is it that you would prefer to solve your problem? The employee who is standing in front of you, his supervisor, the manager of the department, the general manager or perhaps the president of the company? Well, in the very vast majority of cases, the answer is going to be the employee who is standing in front of you.

Let me give you some cases in point so as to underline how ridiculous the absence of empowerment can be:

> You ask a housemaid in a hotel for some extra towels and she tells you that she can't give them to you unless the supervisor authorises it!
> You arrive one minute late at MacDonald's for breakfast and the staff at the counter tells you they can no longer serve the breakfast menu because it's not allowed!
> An employee at a hotel reception tells you he can't take the charge off of your bill for the peanuts that they claim you have consumed from the minibar (which you didn't) unless his front office supervisor says he can!

This would be particularly embarrassing if the guest has just spent 4000 dollars in your hotel and comes to your hotel five times a year.

As you can see, it would probably be best to let the employees take decisions in all of the preceding situations (even by using good old common sense). This also leads to the conclusion that empowerment is all about **giving permission to make decisions.**

From the diagram on page 25 , you can see that confidence, training and empowerment are closely related.

In order for employees to be given your confidence (trust) and to be confident in making decisions, they need to be well trained for the job that they are doing. As far as empowerment goes, it is also important to ensure that the employees know to what extent they have the power to make decisions (for example, not to cancel a hotel bill for three nights because the guest complains that the air conditioning is not working correctly)!

Empowerment is all about creating the right conditions so that your employee is not only competent to make certain decisions but also knows that he has your trust to do so!

I would define empowerment as follows:

Employee empowerment is about giving employees your trust so that they have the confidence to take decisions in the workplace without supervision.

Of course, there has been a lot of talk around this subject for a long time and the problem is that in a lot of organisations this is talked about but not put in place.

This is such a shame but the good news is that, if you do this, it will give you yet another potential source of competitive advantage!

Now that your employees are expressing themselves, or at least have been given "permission" to express themselves, and the **right conditions** have been **created** to allow them to do so and they have been **empowered** to be more involved in the decision-making processes in the operational part of the business, it's now time to look at **taking on board their ideas!**

In the following section, we will discuss just why this is terribly important and what can be done to ensure that ideation becomes the norm within the organisation (as opposed to the exception).

Remember there is **no such thing as a bad idea.** The important thing is whether or not it is relevant to what you are doing or plan to do in the company and then, of course, whether or not you decide to do it is another thing entirely!

Also, in allowing more room for **employee expression** and **empowerment,** you are not only creating the **conditions for** the **success** of your **employees** but also of the **organisation.**

EMPLOYEE IDEAS

YOU NEED TO TAKE ON BOARD EMPLOYEE IDEAS

Why is this so <u>very important</u>?

Just think about the last time that you **had a great idea** about how to make your company more successful and were completely **ignored by your direct superior** or even higher up in the "food chain". It might very well have been an idea that **could have made the company loads of money or profits.**

In addition to all of this, and **to add insult to injury,** no one has bothered to take the time to explain to you why this is a bad idea or why it is not possible to put in place.

The results of this are likely to be as follows:

➤ You are probably feeling very frustrated by this.
➤ You might go from being a very happy employee to a very unhappy one.
➤ You certainly won't be sharing any more bright ideas.
➤ You might even leave the company where you are working and share this bright idea with your future employer.

Well, all this goes to show that, once again, the company will lose valuable employees and ideas like this if management continues to ignore ideas generated by their employees. Not only that but, as mentioned before, this might also lead to higher turnover than is normal for the organisation and therefore incur unnecessary recruitment and training costs.

So in summary:

YOU NEED TO LISTEN TO IDEAS GENERATED BY YOUR EMPLOYEES.

This does not mean that you always need to take on board ideas coming from your employees as they may not always be good ideas or, in some cases, may be impossible to put in place. But you should listen to ideas and give feedback as to whether the ideas are good or not.

You never know: maybe one day one of these ideas will **fundamentally change the way that the organisation is doing business!**

Let's say that an employee has had a game changing idea and passed this on to you. This is great news and, so as to ensure that this behaviour is reinforced in the right way, please really don't do the following:

"SAY THAT IT WAS YOUR IDEA TO MAKE YOURSELF LOOK GOOD!"

If the idea that came from the employee was truly awesome, it might be tempting to do this. However, the results of doing this will be truly disastrous because it will be much more difficult in future to encourage employees to share ideas and, apart from that, in doing so you will definitely damage your own and the company's reputation.

On the contrary, the employee should be given credit and recognition and even be rewarded for coming up with this idea. This in turn should and will very probably lead to the further generation of ideas from your employees.

<u>Positive reinforcement can be a truly powerful tool!</u>

PASS ON IMPORTANT MESSAGES

Now that you are starting to take on board some of the great ideas that you are getting from your employees and you are on speaking terms with them, why not use this as a golden opportunity to "get across" to them.

It does not matter whether you are in a one-to-one situation or speaking to groups of employees, it is always important to get across key messages for and on behalf of the organisation.

This can be really very simple indeed. Imagine you meet one of the most influential of your employees at the coffee machine and say to him, for example:

"Remember the Employee Survey that we carried out, some great news. We have the results and it's showing us that we have some great opportunities for improvement . . ."

This is only an example but don't worry: if the **employee** is as **influential** as he is supposed to be, the whole organisation will know about this **positive message** ten minutes later!

One very important way to pass or transmit a powerful message to your employees is to **act on what you have been told by the employees.** This is, after all, what it means to take on board their ideas.

I will underline once again that this does not mean that every idea coming from employees is a good one or that it is possible to put it in place.
However, what is crucial is that when you do put in place one of these ideas, make sure that you remember to pass on the message OR say:

"YOU TOLD US. WE DID IT!"

And remember to give credit to the employees concerned and underline how important this is for the future of the organisation.

The last part of why recognition is so important is about the **importance of communication** for your company. Read on . . .

TO IMPROVE COMMUNICATION

So far, we have looked at the importance of the following areas as to why employee recognition is so very important:

> - To show employees that you care
> - To find out how they feel
> - To take on board their ideas
> - To let them express themselves
> - To pass on important information

As we saw from the diagram about why it is so important to listen to employees, the reasons are both multiple and interdependent.

But, as we all know, communication can be a highly complex affair especially in a large organisation. Like a lot of things, however, **it can be made very simple.**

Most organisations and companies can be split into two broad categories: those that are structured vertically and those that are structured horizontally.

But it really doesn't matter that much, **does it?**

What **is important,** on the other hand, is that the communication links between each part of the organisation remain open and efficient.

Look at the following:

Interesting, yes?

If you are in an organisation where communication is mainly vertical this could be represented on the diagram you will see on the next page.

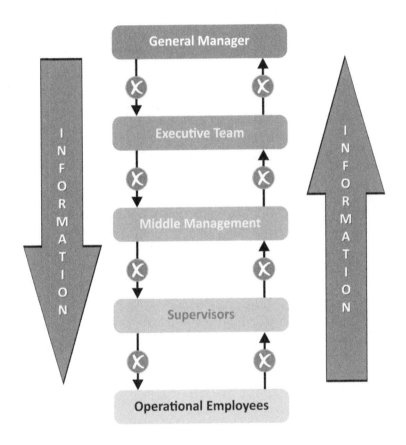

From the diagram on the previous page, two things are immediately obvious:

1. Communication flows both ways from the top down and from the bottom up.
2. If, at any stage in this process, there is a "breakdown" in communication (represented by the crosses), the consequences for the company can be catastrophic.

Let's take an example where there is a breakdown both ways between the executive team and the middle management of the company. Let's say that the executive team thinks that employee engagement and employee power are strategically important for the organisation.

However, it would seem that they have **not** been able to **convince middle management,** who are not only reticent but are **not supporting the strategy**.

WHY MIGHT THIS BE, DO YOU THINK?

There could be any number of reasons, amongst them some of the following:

> ➢ Middle management believes that they themselves are not treated well or fairly by the organisation.
> ➢ No one asked them their opinion about this (they did not participate in making the strategy).
> ➢ The executive team never listens to their ideas on this particular subject.
> ➢ There is a lack of exemplarity from the executive team with regards to the way employees are treated.

And the list goes on. The real point here is that even if top management are convinced that this is the right way to go, they are highly unlikely to succeed if middle management is not advocating the same strategy.

It would seem fairly obvious from this example that if middle management is not convinced, they will not transmit the message correctly or even at all to the junior management of the operational employees.

Hence, a complete breakdown in communication across the organisation!

Now imagine that a company was having this kind of problem at every stage of the communication process on our diagram.

This would of course lead to **complete chaos** in the organisation as no one would know what they were meant to be doing (or giving priority to) and conflicting messages would be going up and down the communication chain. Said another way:

COMMUNICATION WILL ONLY BE AS GOOD AS THE WEAKEST LINK IN THE CHAIN!

Yet another way of looking at this is to compare communication to the game Chinese Whispers! We all know what can happen to the message at the start of this game when you compare it to the message at the end.

In case it wasn't obvious, we have been talking here about mostly **verbal communication,** but written communication is obviously also important particularly when you look at the volume of emails which are produced in organisations today.

When writing to or receiving emails from other employees in the organisation, I believe that we all share some of the same thoughts such as:

> ➢ Why am I on copy on this mail, it has absolutely nothing to do with me?
> ➢ Should I write a mail or just call the guy?
> ➢ Who should I copy in on this mail?
> ➢ Who should I send the mail to and who should be on copy?
> ➢ Why is the guy in the office next to mine writing to me?

The point here is not to answer the questions above but only to say that **if you are having doubts about sending a mail, it's probably best not to do it**. Or, at the very least, take your time before sending replies and think about your answer before you reply.

As we all know, **emails** can lead to some terrible **misunderstandings** and can be **interpreted** quite easily as being **unimportant** (because you receive so many), **unclear** (because they are badly written) or even, in some cases, **darn right rude**.

The point that I'm making here is **not to stop using emails** (although I believe that less is better/or less is more), but to ensure that this **tool** is **used correctly** in the organisation in order to **enhance** and **improve communication** between the employees and **not,** on the contrary, to **destroy it**.

We'll talk more later in the book about how to improve verbal and written communication.

Now that we have just about covered **why employees** are so **important** to the company or organisation and we have some clues about **where to start,** we need to get down to "brass tacks", meaning how are you going to **use** all of that **potential** as a real **power source** on the road to **employee power!**

Chapter Five

How to Increase Employee Power

Increasing Employee Power

PLANS FOR INCREASING EMPLOYEE POWER

In Chapters Two to Four, we discussed why being more employee centric and recognising employees is so important for an organisation. Hopefully, you agree by now why this is so crucial!

But what exactly are you going to do about it and how are you going to do it? Probably the best place to start is to "plan your work and work your plan". This may sound a little glib until you think about the following phrase and its importance:

"Proper Planning Prevents Poor Performance"

You could also put a sixth P in here somewhere but I'll leave it up to you to guess what it is and put it in yourself!☺

Seriously, though, planning is important and, in this chapter, I will put forward some ideas about a plan which will definitely help you to unleash all of this power!

Having another look at the diagram on page 48, which explains the main points as to why employee power is so important, would be an excellent starting point.

Below, I have taken the liberty of placing the same diagram, together with some numbered annotations. **Don't worry, you will see why I have done this immediately afterwards!**

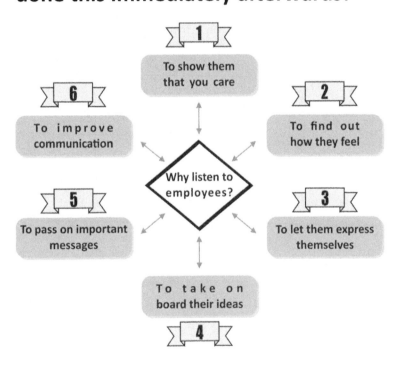

On the diagram, you can see that I have numbered from one through six each of the areas as to why it is so important to listen to employees. I have done this because we will be using this as the foundation of the plan that we will be putting together as to what we are going to do and how we are going to increase employee power within the organisation.

In order to treat each of these areas, I have come up with the following areas that you should work on, namely:

- ➢ **TRAINING**
- ➢ **INTERACTIONS**
- ➢ **MEETINGS**
- ➢ **EMPLOYEES**

This is extremely easy to remember as a mnemonic and it is not an accident that it spells **TIME**. After all, as we all know, **"time is money"**. However, I would argue once again that **if** you **don't use enough time** on these four areas, you are going to **lose** a lot of time and **money in the future**.

Expressing this in a different form gives us:

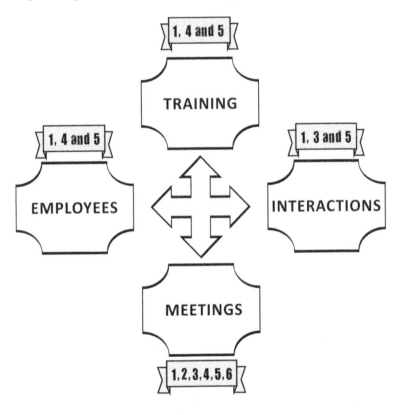

From the diagram on page 80 we have the following:

1. Show them that you care
2. Find out how they feel
3. Let them express themselves
4. Take on board their ideas
5. Pass on messages
6. Improve communication

Each of these numbers is used in the above diagram to show where they are relevant.

In order to clarify, if we were to take Training from the previous page, the fact that we have 1, 4 and 5 associated with it, means that showing employees that you care, taking on board their ideas and improving communication has a significant impact.

If we were then to take Meetings, you can see that it significantly affects all six areas.

Each of the four areas of TIME can positively affect employees' perceptions of where they work and increase their engagement with the company. If your employees are engaged in a positive way with the company, they will be a great source of power.

Let's start by looking at **Training** and seeing what exactly can be done through training your **employees** to **increase** their **engagement** with the company and indeed to make them **more effective!**

Read on!

Chapter Six

Training

Training

Training employees is a vast subject and it is not the purpose of this book to look at every aspect of training and the various methods of training which exist.

The purpose here is to **indicate** some of the **ways** in which **training** can be **effective** and give **results** for the organisation!

Let me ask you a question before we start:

Have you ever been in a training session where you have had some of the following thoughts?

"What am I doing here?"
"What is the purpose of this training?"
"What a waste of my time!"
"This is utterly boring!"
"Can't wait for the damn coffee break."

If you have not had any of these thoughts, during training, you have probably attended some very high quality training or at the very least training which you found interesting!

If, on the other hand, you have had these kinds of thoughts, you were **not motivated** for the training in question for some reason, the **subject material did not interest** you or the **training was not well delivered.**

If we take each of the three reasons for having a negative perception of training:

> If you are not motivated, it could be because no one asked you whether or not you wanted to go to this training. It could also be because you do require and need training but not this particular training. Even worse it could be training that is too similar to training that you have already received!

> Quite simply the subject material was of no use to you!

> Perhaps the person doing the training did not do a good job (seemed bored or even worse did not know their subject!)

Whatever the reason might be, there are simple precautions to take when organising training within your company.

When selecting training for your employees, one of the very first things to establish is what are the <u>training needs of the employees</u> or, to put it another way, what are the <u>training priorities of the organisation?</u>

There are simple ways of collating information which will tell you where the training priorities are, such as:

> What are the most common complaints regarding service from your customers.

> Use your employee appraisals/evaluations to establish where exactly your employees require training.

Taking the first of these, if the majority of your customers are telling you that your staff are unfriendly or rude and you are getting very bad comments on Trip Advisor, in this regard, perhaps one of your priorities might be **customer service training!**

From the second point, what if you discovered that most of your employees did not know what the emergency procedures were in the event of a fire! Or that a lot of your employees feel uncomfortable with Spanish guests at the reception area because their Spanish is not good enough.

If your biggest segment of direct customers is Spanish, it would seem like a very big priority to get some Spanish language training put in place.

Now that you have established which training area is a priority for your employees and the organisation, you next need to see **who** is going to carry out the necessary training? Here, the choice is quite simply enormous. However, do ask yourselves the following questions:

- ➤ Do you have internal resources to carry out the training?
- ➤ Is it necessary to use external resources to carry out this particular training and, if so, do you know any companies that have successfully delivered training for your organisation in the past?

Once you have decided who is going to do the training, you now have to decide which training is the most important for the organisation in terms of priorities. An example of this would be the following.

Let's pretend that you are running a very busy restaurant and that you have just had a visit from the hygiene authorities, who tell you that you have a limited time to ensure the conformity of your kitchens and, if this is not done within the limit given, the authorities may decide to close your restaurant! At the same time, you have a very large number of complaints from your customers concerning customer service.

Putting priorities on these two training needs seems quite obvious in terms of the training that needs to take place. However, it's not always that easy to decide. Let's take another example where there appear to be two main training needs for the reception staff at a big hotel: one has been defined as the need for better and quicker use by employees of the Front Desk IT system and the other is customer complaints handling, which none of your reception staff seem to be comfortable with.

If your customer feedback (from whatever source) is telling you that the vast majority of complaints are coming from extremely long check in times and problems with waiting at check out, you can see what the answer here might be!

Once you have established what the training needs and priorities for your employees are, you next need to look at the following questions:

- ➤ What type of training?
- ➤ Who is going to do the training?
- ➤ When are you going to carry out the training?
- ➤ How are you going to do the training?

What type of training is asking several questions at once in order to determine the **pertinence** of the method used? There are of course a variety of choices here such as should the training be done on a one-to-one basis (for example coaching or mentoring)? Should the training be carried out in a classroom situation or would on-the-job training perhaps be more effective?

Of course you can see that when you start to ask some of these questions, they can easily lead on to yet other questions.

In order to help you to start answering these questions, have a look at the diagram on the following page:

INTEGRATION

Before looking at each of the areas from the previous page, there is one particular area of training which merits special attention and, if not done at all or done badly, can have terrible consequences for any organisation, namely integration.

The first few days or weeks for an employee when he starts a new job can be extremely stressful. You probably all know what I'm talking about here as you've more than likely been through some of this at some stage in your career. I know I have.

When the employee arrives, remember that he/she doesn't know anyone, does not know his/her way around, doesn't know the "rules" and certainly doesn't have a clue about the "company culture".

If you don't have an integration programme or training in place, it would be a priority to get one put in place quick!

A good integration programme should contain most of the following elements:

> - An introduction to colleagues and the hierarchy.
> - A guided tour of the premises where he/she will be working.
> - Organised "one-to-one" meetings with the colleague with whom he/she will be working the most often.
> - Written materials explaining how the organisation works to include:
>   - An organisation chart for the company.
>   - Rules and regulations of the workplace.
>   - Company culture.
> - **Assigning a mentor to the new employee.**

In a perfect world, you might envisage a two-day integration training programme which talks about the history and culture of your company. Indeed, a lot of larger organisations take this approach. Nevertheless, don't forget that the integration process is just that, a process, and should take as long as is necessary to **ensure** that the new **employee feels welcome** and **comfortable** in his or her new work environment.

This is one of the reasons why assigning a mentor to the new employee is such a good idea. After all, not everyone is able to assimilate all of the information regarding their new job and workplace within the first week!

Let's say for the sake of argument that you assign a mentor to your new employee for the first three months that he or she is with the company. This will give the employee the opportunity to ask questions and integrate more easily with his/her colleagues. One very important issue is, of course, that the employees who are mentors should themselves be highly engaged with the company and enthusiastic in their role as mentor. If possible, the mentor should undergo formal training for this role; at the very least, there should be a set of guidelines and/or **best practice** for mentors in place.

One very obvious way to train **future mentors** is to have your **most successful mentors train others**. In that way, you should be able to ensure that the guidelines/best practices are passed on correctly.

I am nearly sure that you as an employer or manager do not want to lose too much time with new **employees** who are either **not productive** or doing **very poor quality work**!

As an example, let's imagine that you own a hotel and that you have just hired some new cleaners for the rooms. If the maids who are there already are all cleaning 10 rooms per day, what do you think will happen if you ask the new maids to also clean 10 rooms on their first day at work?

I think you can easily see what the answer might be here!

The point that I am making here is that if you do not properly integrate your employees, you risk having employees who leave quickly and cause a loss of time and money (increased recruitment, turnover and training costs) or, if they do stay, there is a risk that they will be poorly engaged with the company.

<u>Integrating employees correctly is an investment for now and the future.</u>

Let's now have a look at the elements from page 92, starting off with on-the-job training.

ON-THE-JOB TRAINING

On the job training is exactly what it says it is, training whilst doing the job in question. Another way of putting this is that the employee(s) in question will be **learning by doing!**

This is a great way for employees to learn provided that it is done in the right way. So what is the right way? Well, to start with, you have to create the right conditions and two areas that have to be considered in order to do this are as follows:

> ➢ How long should the training last?
> ➢ Who should do the training?

Obviously, for the first of these questions, the training should last as long as necessary so that the employee becomes proficient in whatever the task being trained is.

This may seem obvious but, so as to ensure that it is, let's take an example. Let's say that you want to train a receptionist to do check ins and check outs at a hotel.

Say that you decide to put the employee in a real situation immediately in front of the guest and tell the other receptionists to "keep an eye" on the new recruit. This would probably turn out to be either a very long or a very short process: short because the receptionist is not likely to stay very long in these conditions or, if you are lucky, very long due to the fact that they are not "being trained" and are learning on their own.

I would suggest that, before the employee gets anywhere near the guest, we have to first ensure that they have had sufficient technical training on the computer system. I would then suggest that, after this training, you should not expect the receptionist to be able to complete the same number of check ins and/or check outs as an experienced receptionist.

You should have a standard to decide after what amount of time the receptionist should become autonomous: is it four days, two weeks or a month? Let's imagine that we have decided that after their technical training, a receptionist will have a sufficient amount of autonomy after two weeks.

Let's also say that you have decided to give him a mentor who will be responsible for "showing him the ropes". Furthermore, you have decided that you are going to use your "best" receptionist to accompany your new recruit (that is to say, the receptionist who is well known for doing the fastest check ins/outs and who also has great guest feedback.
Unfortunately, you discover after the two weeks that your new recruit wants to leave!

Why might that be? After all, he has had his technical training and we have given him a mentor; **everything should be all right, no?**

Well, it could be because you forgot to ask the mentor that you chose if he was interested in being a mentor or, even more likely, you forgot to train the mentor on job training skills/techniques or maybe you did not even give the mentor a checklist of items to go through with his/her trainee.

One of the best ways to ensure that your on-the-job trainers are going to be effective is to make it voluntary or put a selection process in place so as to ensure that mentors are happy to take on this role. Your on-the-job trainers need to be:

> Enthusiastic about taking on this role.
> Given precise objectives on what needs to be trained for.
> Trained in the basic techniques of on-the-job training.

Before speaking about the technique for on-the-job training, do remember **that it is not because an employee is the best at his job that he will make the best trainer!**

As to the technique that on-the-job trainers should be using, it should be based on the following principles:

> **Show** your trainee how the task to be done is carried out step by step.
> **Ask** the trainee to carry out the task and monitor his performance.
> **Feedback** given to the employee. Let him/her try it again if necessary.
> **Employee** should then show you how the task is done step by step.

And, no, it's not a mistake that the above statements give a mnemonic which spells SAFE:

Show the employee how it's done

Ask the employee to do it

Feedback given to the employee

Employee shows you how to do it

On-the-job training should be one of the cornerstones of any company's training plan. Nevertheless, you really need to remember and apply the basics so that it is effective in enhancing employee engagement:

> - **On-the-job training to be structured both in terms of time and content.**
> - **On-the-job trainers to be properly selected.**
> - **On-the-job trainers to be trained to apply the SAFE method.**

Now, let's go on to look into classroom training!

CLASSROOM TRAINING

Classroom training is of course exactly what it says it is – training that takes place with a group of people in a classroom situation/training room.

As with on-the-job training, we should also take a look at how long the training should last and who should carry out the training.

If you have people within the organisation who are already qualified trainers, this is of course good news. If not and you have experts in the subject areas to be covered, you really do have to ensure that they **have been trained as a trainer**.

If you don't, you run the risk of having an **expert** to train people who has absolutely **no idea how to transmit or share his knowledge**.

As to how long the training needs to (or should) last, **DON'T BE STINGY!!**

Throughout my working life, I have often heard things such as "we can't afford him/her to go on training for such a long period" or "they're going to be absent from work for too long" or even, yes, you've guessed: "time is money!"
All very true; but, and it's a big **BUT:**

IF YOU DON'T *SPEND* THE TIME NOW, IT WILL *COST* YOU MORE IN THE FUTURE!

You could, of course, try and argue the above point but wouldn't it be pointless to take the risk of not spending long enough (or enough money) training your people?

As a case in point, if your people stay within the company and are not well trained, you will probably find that there will be costly mistakes and lower productivity, both of which lead of course to **decreasing profit margins.**

I think the following really drives the message home:

Chief Financial Officer says to the Chief Operating Officer:

"What if we spend all of this money on training our employees and they leave?"

Chief Operating Officer replies:

"What if we don't spend any money and they stay?"

I don't think we need to spend any more time at this point underlining just how important it is to give adequate time to training your employees.

Let's go on now to speak about the different types of training that might take place within the classroom or training room.
Here, you should take some time to decide whether or not you want your training to be highly participative?

Of course, certain subjects such as IT training, technical subjects or training for obligatory certification are not all that participative by nature (although a good course structure and trainer can make them more so).

My advice would be to make your training **as participative as possible**. It's not only a great way to learn but it also keeps the attention levels of the participants high throughout (and here I am talking from experience).

One great way of training is through what people now call group coaching (basically brainstorming). The subject of this book is not to go into the various techniques of brainstorming, although there are some basic rules which I feel are important to share with you.

Brainstorming sessions should be planned in the following way:

- ➢ Ensure that the subject is clearly defined.
- ➢ Ensure that everyone participates.
- ➢ Remember that there is no such thing as a bad idea.
- ➢ Write the ideas down as you go along.
- ➢ Group ideas which are similar together.
- ➢ Once the generation of ideas is complete, regarding the subject, get the group to vote in a hierarchy (say the best ideas from one to ten).

Once you have the hierarchy of ideas, you have the subject matter for your training (unless of course the point of the training was to teach people how to brainstorm)!

Of course, you don't have to go as far as brainstorming to get your employees participating.

For example, let's say that the training is about the importance of the quality of the guest experience and that you are in a service sector industry.

You could have a number of open discussions within the group during the course of the training by posing questions to the group such as:

> - Why is the quality of the guest experience so important?
> - What is the most important thing regarding the guest experience for our business?
> - How are we going to improve guest services in our company?

Not only is asking the right question a great way to get participants to engage during the training, it is also a great way to generate ideas which may have a major positive impact for the company. In addition, it is also a fantastic way of increasing employee engagement with the company.

INTERNAL VERSUS EXTENRAL RESOURCES

Now that we have touched on on-the-job and classroom training, let's have a look at the choice regarding the use of internal versus external resources in a bit more detail: Indeed, you might find that it will turn out cheaper in the long run to use an outside company for some of your training requirements due to the fact that you won't waste time creating training, making mistakes and taking the risk of badly-delivered training. All of which would obviously lead to an end result that you really don't want.

Remember good training companies are there to give you advice and this can save you a lot of time and money in the long run.

However, like everything else not all training companies are at the same level of excellence. So, make sure that you get the best for your most valuable asset (your employees).

So, how can you ensure that you get a good training company? Well here are some good places to start:

> Ask around to colleagues, people you know, employees and competitors.
> Look at how various companies are reviewed on the internet.
> Meet a selection of companies and talk to them.

Whatever mix of **internal** and **external** resources you decide to use, do remember that they are **not mutually exclusive.**

Before moving on to discuss the importance of interactions in the workplace, really do "take on board" the quote below as this will send you on the path to powering up your employees through training!

CONCLUSIONS

To conclude the section on training, I would like to share a quote from Richard Branson, which really does speak for itself:

"Train your people well enough so that they can leave and then treat them well enough so that they don't."

Richard Branson

Chapter Seven

Interactions

Interactions

If you go back to the diagram on page 80, we underlined the following main reasons for the importance of interactions with your employees:

- ➤ Show them that you care.
- ➤ Let them express themselves.
- ➤ Pass on affirmative messages.

Before looking at each of these areas in a little more detail, I would just underline that **every single interaction** that you have with your employees is **important** whether it's totally informal (at the coffee machine) or in a structured meeting discussing the current and future strategy of the company.

Show them that you care

Let's imagine that you meet one of your employees at the coffee machine and that he tells you he is extremely happy because his first child has been born! It could be a great idea to send your congratulations by way of a hand-written card congratulating him and his partner on this event. And why not go the whole way and send some flowers to his partner/wife with the card!

I hear you say that you have never seen this done in a company for which you have worked. Well, for me, that is another great reason to do it. If you consider your **employees** to be your **most valuable resource**, remember that there is always competition for valuable resources so make sure that you **stay ahead of the competition**!

Apart from anything else, this example shows that you listened to the employee and, even more importantly, that you took some action.

Let employees express themselves:

Let's imagine, here, that you have organised an open forum in the form of a breakfast meeting with some of your shop floor employees. Let's further say that this has been organised to last for a period of two hours and that you have set things up so that they will have a great breakfast experience (coffee, orange juice, fresh croissants and a full English breakfast).

Well, so far, this looks great and you are certainly making an effort to show them that you care.

Until that is that you have spent two hours talking (and eating!) and telling them about how lucky they are to work for such a great company and at the same time have not given them time to ask any questions!

In fact, in this situation just described, although they might indeed be happy with the breakfast, you may just have **caused** a huge amount of **frustration** amongst them. How would you feel if you had been invited to this and spent a lot of time preparing questions for the "boss" only to find that there was **no time to ask** any of your **questions**?

So do make sure that your employees have time to ask questions during this type of forum and that they know in advance so that they have time to prepare them.

But, and it's a big BUT, don't feel obliged to answer all of the questions that you are asked immediately.

If you are not sure of the response to a question, note it down and let them know how and when you will get back to them on this subject (and then make sure that you do).

This is extremely important. If you do give a wrong answer to something during this type of meeting or you do not get back to them with an answer as promised, this may well lead to a lack of confidence in leadership/management.

This is obviously not what you are looking to achieve here.

In order to avoid this type of situation, why not take notes or have someone also take notes during the breakfast and, of course, let them know that you are taking notes and why you are taking them.

Passing on important messages

This type of breakfast forum might also be a good time to pass on a certain number of important messages or to reinforce messages that you think have already been transmitted by senior or middle management.

When welcoming the participants to the meeting, you can give an introductory speech explaining why it is important to ask any questions that the participants might have and letting them know that this is their meeting.

You could then pass on some important messages to the employees. This might be, for example, to tell them about positive guest quality survey results, to talk about some basic financial information or to take the opportunity to stop a nasty and destructive rumour that the company is being bought out (particularly, if it's not true).

Going back now to the employees expressing themselves, do make sure that you give them time to express themselves and ask their questions. What I mean here is that they are not always used to speaking in public, so give them time and don't interrupt them unless it's to ensure that you have correctly understood the question.

Remember <u>reformulating</u> someone's question is not only a good way to ensure that you have perfectly understood it, it is also a great way of showing that you have been listening attentively and that you care!

The very fact of using this technique shows that you are paying attention and that you care about what they have to say.

So, in summary, during all of your interactions with your employees, don't hesitate to:

> - Listen attentively;
> - Give them time to ask questions;
> - Reformulate to ensure understanding;

Answer their questions (even with a delay, but make sure that you get back to them).

If you do make a conscious effort to do all of the above, I can assure you that the results will come and that the quality of interpersonal communication within the organisation will steadily improve.

Apart from anything else, you will be setting the stage for more effective communication within the company, as we discussed earlier, and also putting in place some great habits in general.

These so called habits are also important for the next subject for discussion, namely MEETINGS.

Chapter Eight

Meetings

Meetings

There is such an enormous variety of types of meetings and, in some cases, such an enormous number of meetings (you know what I'm talking about, right?) that it's really hard to know where to start with this subject.

I've therefore decided to start with a very simple question:

Why do we hold meetings?

Well the first thing to say here is that there are as many reasons to hold meetings as there are types of meetings. Having said that, there are really two very basic reasons to hold a meeting, which are:

- ➤ **TO SHARE INFORMATION**
- ➤ **TO COMMUNICATE**

Nevertheless, in order to ensure that you share information and communicate both as effectively and efficiently as possible within the organisation, you should put in place a number of rules for holding your meetings. The very first question should always be:

"For a given subject, do we really need to hold a meeting?"

In my experience, we often hold meetings which are unnecessary, which occur too frequently or where the issue could have been solved during a quick telephone or skype call.

I'm pretty sure that you have attended meetings where you have asked yourself: "what am I doing here?", "why was I invited to this particular meeting?", "what has this got to do with me?" or even, in some cases, "what is the subject of the meeting?" I'm also sure that you have attended meetings where you thought "what a total waste of time this is for me!" If this has been the case, please rest assured that the vast majority of participants round the table were probably thinking the same thing!

It seems obvious that if we are wasting time with meetings which are unnecessary, this is not at all employee centric as you are wasting the time of your most important asset when they could be elsewhere being truly productive.

All of this points once again to the question:

DO WE REALLY NEED A MEETING?

Yes, I do realise that I have repeated myself, but it really is so important to get this right whether you are organising a meeting for the first time or considering whether or not to continue with a meeting that is already in place.

In order to ensure that your meetings are effective, the big question is:

WHAT IS THE PURPOSE OF THE MEETING?

To put it simply, if you don't know the answer to this question, don't hold the meeting! More seriously, this underlines the importance of defining precisely what does motivate the necessity of holding a meeting, for example:

> ➢ Is the purpose to pass on important information?
> ➢ To look at how to improve our guest satisfaction scores?
> ➢ To analyse our most recent P&L?
> ➢ To discuss the overall strategy of the company?

This list is by no means exhaustive; the important thing here is that, once you have defined precisely why you need a meeting, you should have precise rules.

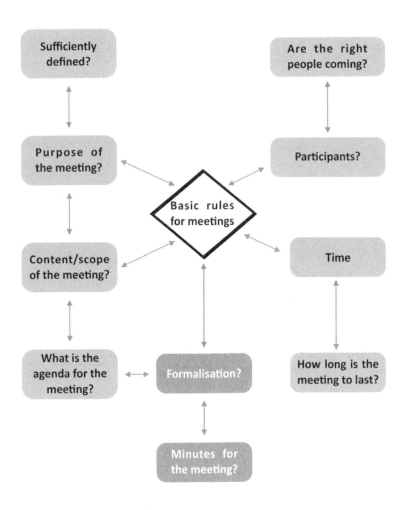

PURPOSE OF THE MEETING

Here, as I said earlier, the important thing is to define precisely **why** we are holding the meeting. Is this a meeting where we are simply sharing information regarding the company's performance? Or is the meeting about ensuring that all of the participants at the meeting understand the information so that **they can cascade this down to other employees**? In other words, are the participants only there to receive the information themselves or should they be sharing the information following the meeting?

Another thing to consider for this meeting would be whether or not the information is to be "given only", or if there is to be debate or a question-and-answer session at the end of the meeting.

What we are saying, at the end of the day, is that the title/introduction of the meeting should really give a very big clue as to its purpose.

As for titles, what do you think of the following titles?

➢ Quality meeting
➢ Quality meeting to discuss satisfaction
➢ Quality meeting to discuss employee satisfaction
➢ Quality meeting to discuss the improvement of employee satisfaction
➢ Quality meeting to discuss how to improve employee satisfaction following on from the most recent employee satisfaction survey results.

If you used the first title, no one knows what we might be discussing (the quality of the physical environment, quality processes, guest satisfaction, and so on).

As we go down this list, you can see that the future participants will have a better and better idea about what is to be discussed and, indeed, in the last title, what the purpose of the meeting actually is. Provided, that is, that they are informed in advance, which brings us to the next point concerning content.

CONTENT/SCOPE OF THE MEETING

Now that we have a purpose for the meeting, we should really define what information is to be shared during the meeting and what exactly should be discussed. Yes, you've guessed we should make an agenda for the meeting and ensure that the future participants of the meeting are informed and, indeed, given the agenda well in advance of the date on which the meeting is to be held.

If we use our previous example, the agenda might look something like this:

> ➤ Presentation of the most recent employee satisfaction survey results
> ➤ Identification of critical areas for improvement
> ➤ Identification of quick wins
> ➤ Action plans (who is to work on which critical area/quick win)
> ➤ Further points
> ➤ Date for the next meeting

If you produce an agenda that looks something like this, then you are well on your way to properly defining the scope of the meeting.

In other words, you have not decided to come up with a global strategy with regard to employee satisfaction, but you have identified critical elements and potential quick wins. You have also decided that the purpose of the meeting is to identify these and to start working on action plans in order to start resolving some of these issues.

You have also decided that further meetings will be necessary to continue this work. So, now that you have decided that you need this meeting and that you have defined the purpose and content of this meeting, just who should you invite to participate?

Well, let's say that we decide to continue with the example of employee satisfaction.

PARTICIPANTS

Since the subject is employee satisfaction and how to improve it, based on the most recent survey results, we might suggest the following list, for example:

- ➤ General Manager
- ➤ Director of Human Resources
- ➤ Training Manager
- ➤ Department heads

In this particular case, we could say (and we would be right) that all department heads should be present due to the fact that employee satisfaction concerns the organisation globally.

On the other hand, if we were discussing problems with a lack of training in the maintenance department, perhaps we might only invite the Training Manager with the Head of Maintenance and the HR Manager? Another example would be if we were discussing IT problems and solutions. Then, we could envisage having a meeting between IT and only the department heads concerned by the problems.

Although, in general, it is extremely important to invite the appropriate participants to meetings (i.e., those who have a direct interest in the subject material for the meeting), don't forget that in some meetings a view from outside can be both pertinent and useful.

For example, let's say that you are discussing the problems with slow check in at the reception and you have been receiving an enormous number of complaints from your guests regarding this.

You might be tempted to call a meeting involving the head of reception together with reception employees to try and solve this issue. Probably a good idea, you say?

Indeed, yes, until you discover that the problem really is that:

> ➤ The printers at reception are too slow and the IT manager is not present.
> ➤ The new recruits have no proper integration programme and no mentor and are taking too long to check the guests in and the HR Manager is not present at the meeting.
> ➤ There is insufficient technical training and the Training Manager is not present.
> ➤ The problem does not come from reception but from housekeeping, who are not providing the cleaned room numbers fast enough to reception and the head housekeeper was not at the meeting.

It's easy to see that this comes back, once again, to defining exactly what the purpose and content of the meeting should be as well as the importance of planning an agenda.

Talking of the agenda, did you notice that there was something missing from the hypothetical agenda on page 125. Yes, that's right: TIME!

TIME

If we use the same agenda from page 125, we should be able to establish the amount of time required for the meeting quite easily. For example, we could plan the meeting as follows:

> Presentation of the most recent employee satisfaction survey results **(20 minutes)**
> Identification of critical areas for improvement **(30 minutes)**
> Identification of quick wins **(10 minutes)**
> Action plans **(who is to work on which critical area/quick win) (10 minutes)**
> Further points **(10 minutes)**
> Date for the next meeting

From the above, your meeting should last no longer than an hour and twenty minutes. Let's say, for the sake of argument that you add in an extra 10 minutes: the **maximum time allowed** for the meeting should be one-and-a-half hours.

However, once you are in the meeting, how do you ensure that we do not go over the planned time? The answer, here, is that you **appoint a timekeeper** for the meeting whose job is to ensure that the **time allocated** for each part of the meeting on **the agenda** is duly **respected.**

This is all to do with planning your work and then working your plan.

Another important thing not to forget is to plan the frequency at which recurring meetings should take place.

Let's say, now, that you have had your meeting and that all has taken place according to the agenda. You were happy with the meeting and there was a good level of participation from all around the table. You could say at this point that you **have had a successful meeting!**

However, in order to ensure that your meeting is effective, there is still one stage missing, namely **formalisation.**

FORMALISATION

Formalisation is important and basically means that minutes should be taken for the meeting and sent to the participants.

The minutes should be as short and concise as possible whilst ensuring that important information is not lost in transcription. I would strongly recommend naming a scribe for each meeting and this is often better if it is someone that knows how to do this professionally (such as an executive assistant).

I would further recommend that you always use the same format so that participants can easily find and use the information contained in the minutes.

The minutes are even more crucial if the meeting is to be recurring (i.e., not a one-off meeting). This is because employees need to know what is expected of them in preparation for the next meeting – for example, the action plans mentioned from our hypothetical meeting on employee satisfaction.

If it is not clearly written who is going to follow up on which quick win or who is going to investigate further the critical areas in order to come up with action plans, this will definitely lead to confusion for the next meeting (and you will lose valuable time sorting this out).

Two last points about the minutes:

The **names** of all of the **participants** as well as the **date** and **time** of the meeting should always appear on the minutes.

For a regular or **recurring meeting,** the **date** of the **next meeting** should be determined at the current meeting and the **minutes** for the meeting should be given to the participants **well in advance of the next meeting.**

Now, are we finished with the basic rules from page 122? Well, as far as the construction of a meeting goes, yes we are! Nevertheless, there are still some very important **<u>rules about running the meeting.</u>**

BASIC RULES FOR MEETINGS

Now that we know how to construct and organise useful meetings, and so as to ensure that our meetings are as productive as possible, we need to look at basic rules for running our meetings.

The basic rules for meetings are as follows:

> - Stick to the agenda
> - Identify roles for the participants
> - Don't interrupt others when they are speaking
> - Phones should be switched off during the meeting
> - No computers should be allowed (except when used for the presentation itself)

Sticking to the agenda means talking about the subjects on the agenda and sticking to the time allocated for each (as just discussed earlier).

We did not, however, discuss identifying roles for a certain number of participants within the meeting, so let's do that now!

The main roles which need to be attributed in order to run a successful meeting are the following:

> - Chairman
> - Timekeeper
> - Scribe

The timekeeping role is obvious and we discussed this earlier. The scribe is also obvious as this is the person who takes notes during the meeting and prepares the minutes.

The chairperson is the person who is running the meeting and who is in charge of ensuring that the various points on the agenda are addressed and who also ensures that the "rules" are respected during the meeting (such as participants not interrupting each other).

There is more to say regarding this important role. In your opinion, should it always be the same employee who chairs the meeting?

I believe that the answer to this question should be no. If we are serious about increasing employee engagement, what better way of doing this than allowing each of them in turn the opportunity to chair the meeting!

I have done this in the past and it has proved extremely effective. I believe the reason for this, like a lot of things is, that you are **demonstrating** your **confidence in your fellow employees** and thereby enhancing their motivation and engagement with the company.

To further enhance the *employee-centric nature* of your *meetings,* why not ask *participants to propose subjects* for the agendas of *future meetings*?

And, now, let's get down to the debate on whether phones and computers should be allowed in meetings?
I believe that the answer to this question in the vast majority of cases should be a very **big NO!**

As a case in point, have you ever tried to talk to an adolescent whilst he is in another virtual reality (translation when he/she is looking at their phone). If you have had this experience, I think you might agree that the results, in terms of a good, healthy and communicative exchange, rapidly approach zero!

How many times have you been in a meeting where everyone else round the table has their laptop open and is working on it whilst the meeting is in progress! Do you think these employees are being duly attentive to what is actually going on in the meeting or that they are going to contribute something useful? Or perhaps they have all taken on the role of the scribe for the meeting and are taking notes (bit of friendly sarcasm here ☺).

In order to respect each of the participants around the table and ensure that each of them knows that they are important, they should be listened to when they are speaking.

If you are addressing a meeting and no one lifts their head from their computer or phone whilst you are speaking, you are in trouble.

As I said earlier, it's best to have all the phones switched off and not allow computers in the meetings. Although some of your more "techi" or adolescent participants might find this as close to being an "amputation of their virtual body", there is a an old saying that sums this up:

"Sometimes the medicine that tastes the worst is the best for you."

Yes, I do know that this last part regarding electronic devices is fertile terrain for a debate. But, if you still don't believe that I might be right about this, why not try it and see what the results are?

So, in summary for this section on basic rules for planning and holding meetings, remember to think about the following:

> - **Do you need a meeting?**
> - Purpose
> - Content
> - Participants
> - Time
> - Formalisation
> - **Rules for running the meeting**

Now that we've talked about the basic rules on how to prepare and run meetings, let's talk about what types of meetings you should be having and why these meetings are important.

The very first thing that I would say is that meetings should be as participative as possible as there is nothing worse than sitting in a meeting and listening to the same person talking (or "droning" on) about something for two hours. I'm sure that we've all had this experience at one time or another, right?

Remember that meetings of a participative nature do engage your employees more within the meeting but also, and more to the point, with the company or organisation.

So, what can be some of the more important types of meetings within organisations and why are each of them so important for you and your employees?

Let's start by having a look at the diagram on the next page:

This way

MEETINGS FOR INDIVIDUALS

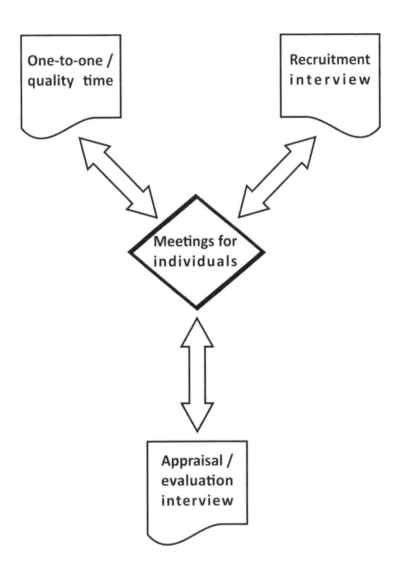

Recruitment Interviews

I think we can all agree that first impressions do count? I think most people would also agree that when someone comes to an interview they are hopefully trying to make a good impression?

But, as an employer, are you sure that you are making the right impression on your future potential employee? This is so important and today, in particular, when the job market is clearly becoming more and more competitive!

Have you ever been to an interview where you were not offered anything to drink, not even a coffee or a glass of water, where the interviewer did not seem to be paying attention to you, had not read your CV or even worse spent the entire interview looking at his telephone or interrupting the interview to go off on a call and then come back?

If you have been through an interview process like this, I'm pretty sure that you were not at all impressed and I'm almost totally sure you probably did not go to work for this company.

You really do need to ensure that you give the future employee the right impression. At the very least, you should do the following:

> Read the CV and take notes about questions you want to ask.
> Welcome the person to the interview.
> Offer them something to drink.
> Give them time to ask questions about the company and/or the post that they are applying for.
> Listen attentively and show interest in what they are saying (and remember what we said about reformulation).

All of the above sounds so simple and common sense that you would think everyone would be doing this, but this is far from being the case! So why not take advantage and put in place a really WOW welcome for your potential employee.

Remember you are competing for your most valuable resources here, namely your employees.

Appraisal/Evaluation Interviews

For a very large number of employees, at whatever level, this is the most important time of the year. This is after all where they will find out what their direct manager thinks of them and of their performance!

Is the above phrase correct? Not really, because we talked about what the manager "thinks" of them.

What the manager should really be aiming at is judging the performance of the employee in their role within the organisation by using criteria which are as objective as possible!

Remember that the appraisal interview is important for your employee and that, not only is it a good time to **give constructive** feedback, it is also very important to **listen** to the employee **attentively** and find out about his or her aspirations.

All appraisal meetings should contain a section which evaluates the **precise competence** of the person as well as a section on **behavioural competence or skills**. There should also be a significant part of the process which talks about **development and training.**

Earlier in the book, we discussed the importance of putting in place a training plan for the company which is both effective and relevant. An appraisal process is a great place to start with the identification of training needs whether they are individual or more generic.

Also, during the appraisal process, remember that although your **employee** is a member of your team or teams, he/she **is first and foremost an individual** and should be treated as such.

One good tip which I have found works well in preparing an appraisal, is to ask the employee to self-evaluate themselves and give you this evaluation before the meeting takes place. This has a number of advantages such as:

> Quickly identifying where you agree and disagree with this evaluation.
> Clearly identifying where there are valuable points for discussion.
> Getting an idea about your employee's aspirations before the meeting in terms of training needs and wants and ambitions regarding future development.

In summary, this really helps prepare the ground for a successful meeting. In addition, from my experience, it is always good to proceed in this way whether the employee is under-performing, average or a high performer.

Furthermore, whatever level of performance your employee is currently at, the appraisal meeting is an excellent place to discover the reasons for the overall performance of the person and take remedial action should this prove necessary.

This meeting is therefore a golden opportunity to get under- and high-achievers on the road to increasing levels of employee engagement and employee power either through measures designed to reinforce performance which is already good or to help under-achievers to achieve more!

At the end of this meeting, it is crucial to have agreement from the employee on where his strong and weak points lie and where the areas for improvement and development are. And, in some cases, to congratulate the employee on a great performance over the course of the year!

This is all well and good but is it enough to have an appraisal interview with your employee once a year?

The answer is **of course not!**

During the appraisal meeting, you should have clearly identified areas for future improvement, training needs and clear goals and objectives for the year to come.

With regard to the objectives, some may be short term and others more long term (over the course of the year). The goals that **should have been agreed** on should, of course, be smart:

> **S**imple **and S**pecific
> **M**easureable
> **A**greed and **A**ttainable
> **R**elevant
> **T**imed

If any part of SMART from above does not apply to the objectives that you have **agreed upon with the employee,** I would strongly suggest that you have to look at and redefine the objective more precisely.

Please do also try and make sure not to give employees goals which are unrealistic (or just darn right impossible) as this will only lead to loss of confidence in management, de-motivation and frustration. It will certainly not lead towards engagement.

Going back to the aspect of time, if you have set objectives over the course of the whole year, are you really going to consider waiting till the same time next year to see whether or not your employee is on course to reach the objective you have set? I certainly hope not and this takes us nicely on to the next subject, which is the one-to-one meeting with employees (or quality time, as it is sometimes called).

One to Ones/Quality Time

Following on from the previous page, it is extremely important to meet with your employees (and more specifically your direct reports) more than once a year. If we take the example of the annual appraisal interview where you have set objectives together with your employee, imagine what might happen during next year's evaluation when, "lo and behold", you discover that he or she has not fulfilled any of his/her objectives!

This would obviously not be any good with the risk that the employee feels that he/she has "failed" and that instead of having a constructive appraisal meeting it turns into a sort of disciplinary interview! Obviously, not a constructive outcome.

In this context, it would be better if you met with your employee at a minimum on a quarterly basis to get an idea of whether or not he or she is in line with the objectives.

This has the distinct advantage of allowing time to "get things back on track". It could be that your employee needs your help in terms of extra resources or advice.

I would say, however, at this stage that meeting individually with your direct reports on a **quarterly basis really is a strict minimum!**

From my own experience, what I have found to be useful is to meet with employees on an individual basis **once a month** for a formal one to one. There are a number of **advantages** to this, such as:

1) Going over objectives.
2) Opportunity to actively listen to your employee, which is important for them.
3) Glean important information as to what is going on "on the shop floor".
4) Building and reinforcing your relationship with your employee.

If we take point 4, I believe that this is crucial for the foundations of building employee engagement and power. I do fundamentally believe the following:

"People work for other people, not for companies."

This is not to say that people (employees) should not engage with the company and won't be proud to work for the company or organisation. What I am saying is that if they feel that they don't want to work for their boss or that their boss really does not care about what they are doing, there is a very real risk that they will not engage with the company in any way, shape or form.

One of the fundamental reasons for a one to one (or quality time) with an employee on a monthly basis is to give them time to express themselves and show that you care. Your employees should be treated as your internal customers.

We all know that for an organisation to function, you need to take **care** of your customers:

Customers
Are
Really
Everything

Giving due care and attention to your employees on a regular basis is therefore extremely important and giving quality time to them on a monthly basis is a very good way to do this.

In order to ensure that these one-to-one meetings are optimal in nature, it is necessary to formalise them in one way or another. There are many ways to do this. The one that I have used in the past and found very useful is called:

SCOP

Sales

Costs

Operations

People

This is a good framework as it gives opportunities for discussion on a large variety of subjects which may or may not be directly related to the objectives of the employee that you are meeting with.

Under sales, you might talk about the sales of the service, company or department or even the personal sales performance of the employee. Costs might be regarding the important ratios for the department in which they are working (cost of sales, food cost, beverage cost, productivity, etc.).

Operations can cover a wide variety of subjects from service issues to project management. People gives the opportunity for the employee to talk about him or herself regarding how he/she is doing with regard to his or her personal training plan and development.

But not only that, it also gives you an opportunity to talk about training and all other topics related to Human Resources in the department where the employee is working.

As to the time allocated to these discussions, I have always found that one hour is a good place to start (and if it runs over because the employee has a lot to say, it's a good sign). I have also found that formalising these meetings is a good idea and, in the past, I have asked employees to write notes from the meetings under the four SCOP headings and to submit these to me well before the next meeting. This, of course, helps to keep future meetings on track and avoids going over ground which has already been covered.

Don't skimp on these meetings; they really are a great investment and will produce great results for you, the employee and the company. Now let's go and have a look at meetings for groups of employees.

MEETINGS FOR GROUPS

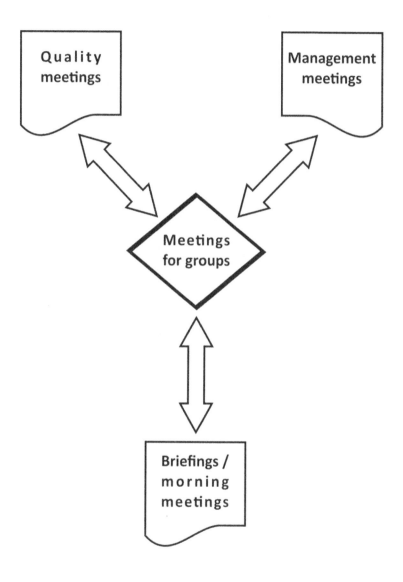

Briefings/Morning Meetings

The first question to ask regarding briefings is what are they for? Well, I would answer this question by saying that their main purpose is to **share information** and, in general, on a **daily basis**.

As an example, operational briefings for the reception of a hotel might look something like:

> ➢ The number of guest arrivals and departures on the day in question.
> ➢ The number of VIPs as well as the room numbers allocated to them.
> ➢ Information regarding the privacy policy for guests.
> ➢ A reminder about a technical issue on the property information system.
> ➢ The weather conditions for the day.

I would also suggest that there are not too many points of information given out during a daily briefing and would further suggest that the briefing should not be too long (10 to 15 minutes should suffice). This is so as to ensure that the information given is retained and put to good use by the employees.

This does not mean that questions should not be asked at the end of the briefing but it does mean that the question and answer section at the end of the briefing should be aimed at the subjects dealt with during the briefing itself.

In short, briefings should be short and to the point!

Quality Meetings

In general, quality meetings exist to discuss and improve the quality of a product or service produced by a company or organisation and can take many forms. Although these meetings can take many forms, they should have at least one thing in common: they should be as participative as possible (unlike briefings, for example).

We all know the expression: "two heads are better than one."

I believe that, in today's highly competitive world, the quality of your service or product is ultra-important. Therefore, it would seem to me that a regular meeting regarding quality and the company's strategy in this respect is crucial to success.

What I have found works well is to have monthly quality meetings (or quality circles) with employees.

As with other meetings, it is important for these meetings to be formalised and, in particular, with the subject to be discussed.

A lot of the time you might find that the subject is too broad.

For example, in one meeting, you might be better to discuss how to solve issues on complaints regarding the queuing time of your customers rather than discussing the overall quality score!

By making these meetings highly participative and ensuring that "the shop floor employees" are present, you might often find that the solution to the problem is found very quickly!

After all, it is very often the person who is actually doing the job who has the key on how to improve it!

As to the techniques to be used and the structure to be given to these meetings, I would further suggest using brainstorming techniques (discussed earlier in the book) as much as possible. An example structure is as follows:

> ➤ Define the area to be discussed for quality improvement.
> ➤ Brainstorm the areas that have been identified as priority.
> ➤ Put in place action plans for the area(s) that have been brainstormed.
> ➤ General discussion of quick wins.
> ➤ Plan the next meeting.

Other types of meetings can also be useful when working on quality-related strategy, such as **open forums**. These are meetings where precise areas for discussion have not been defined (therefore, the opposite of what was suggested above). This type of meeting can be **extremely useful** with regards **to creativity.**

The really good thing about open forums is that the subject is normally more general. For example, you could start the meeting by saying that we are here to discuss levels and types of quality within the organisation and how they relate to one another and leave the discussion "open to the floor".

If you were discussing the above subject, it could lead on to discussions around quality of the product, quality of service, quality of recruitment and training or the identification of the key success factors of the business.
Furthermore, there is a good chance that this type of approach could lead to work on areas that had not

previously been thought about and may be crucial to the future success of your business.

Whatever approach you decide to take, do ensure that it is **highly participative**. I have found in the past that it is much **easier to put in place** ideas which have been **co-generated.**

Management Meetings

First and foremost, what is to be remembered here is that your managers are also employees so that everything that has already been mentioned about the rules for meetings and how to hold them also holds true here.

There are a truly enormous number of subjects that can be covered in management meetings such as finance, HR, operations, projects, and so on.

Nevertheless, the most important thing based on the fact that your **managers** are also **employees** is to make these **meetings as participative as possible**!

When structuring these meetings in the past, I have found the following habits to be useful:

> ➢ When chairing the meeting myself, to give information that concerns everyone at the beginning of the meeting.
> ➢ To allow other managers the opportunity to chair the meeting from time to time (or why not all of the time?)
> ➢ To do a round table so that all managers share information regarding their own department or service.
> ➢ To do a Q&A session at the end of the meeting.

These are, of course, only guidelines but, as you can see from the above, what is really important is that your managers are really involved in the "life" of the meeting as well as the subjects discussed.

Another crucial point to mention here is that the above does not only apply to top management (executive or operations committees). You should really ensure that information and communication flows correctly within the organisation!

One of the best ways of doing this is to ensure that departmental and service meetings are held in the same way.

An even better way to ensure that information is flowing in both directions or being correctly cascaded is for top management to attend departmental and service meetings. One of the easiest things to check here is if the information shared in your executive meetings is reaching other levels within the organisation. If this is not the case, remedial action needs to be taken.

I do firmly believe that if we want maximum employee engagement and power, we need to be sure that all employees at whatever level have the necessary information so as to feel included in the day-to-day success of your company as well as the company's future.

Chapter Nine

Service versus Product

Service versus Product

In spite of the fact that the vast majority (if not all) of the examples used in writing the previous chapters have been taken from the hotel industry, we haven't actually talked about the product itself. In the main part, this is of course due to the fact that it is not really the theme of what we have been writing about.

We should however discuss this in direct relation to what we have been talking about. After all employees do have products to provide, distribute or sell whatever industry they are in and from whatever sector (primary, secondary or tertiary).

So, once again taking hotels as the basis for discussion regarding products, let's ask ourselves the question: what exactly is a hotel?

Well, to start with, it's somewhere that provides accommodation in exchange for payment. It's also somewhere that people (clients or guests) use for a number of different reasons. However, in its simplest expression, the macro segments of your guests are either business or leisure travellers for the most part.

As with our internal clients (your employees), the needs and wants of your clients are evolving constantly and sometimes very rapidly indeed (as is the indeed the case in a lot of other industries).

Nevertheless, in the hotel industry, there are a number of basic needs and wants for clients that have to be met. These basic needs are really quite easy to define in terms of the hotel product itself. I would define these as follows:

> - Bed
> - Breakfast
> - Broadband
> - Bath

Taking these one at a time:

Bed

Well, obviously, when a client pays for a hotel and whether he or she is a business or leisure guest, their primary need is to use the hotel as a place to sleep. Therefore, in the hotel business everything should normally be done so as to ensure that the bed is as comfortable as possible and that the conditions surrounding the "sleeping experience" of the guest are maximal so as to ensure that he or she gets a good rest.

This sounds really easy doesn't it? Well, yes and no! I say this because people also have preferences about how they get their rest. Let me ask you a couple of questions just to push the point home, starting with: have you ever been in a hotel where they provide you with far too many pillows and before you go to sleep at night you end up throwing most of them off the bed so that you can, so to speak, "get your head down"?

Perhaps you might also be someone who switches the air conditioning or heating off in the room before you go to sleep? Only to discover that when you come back to your room for your nights rest that the air conditioning or heating has been put on at "full blast".

On a simpler level, I assume that you like sleeping in a bed that is clean and where there are no hairs on the bed or sheets which are stained and dirty? Do you also like to sleep in a room where there are no nasty odours and that has been correctly aired?

In spite of the fact that the hotel itself may have spent substantial amounts of money on the product itself with a bed and mattress of the highest quality possible and also with bed linen of the highest quality and comfort, the sleeping experience of the guest herself can still go terribly wrong.

Taking each of the examples in turn:

It would be great if you had thrown all of the pillows off of the bed on the first night to discover that care had been taken by the housekeeping employees to replace on the bed only the number of pillows that you had used and that the others had been put aside. A nice surprise indeed! What if they had also put the air conditioning and heating at the same levels you preferred had aired the room correctly and that your bed sheets were not only stain free and impeccably clean but that the linen itself had been properly softened and felt great against your skin when you were sleeping.

Imagine now taking this even further and that you had just happened to mention to an employee during the day that you always slept best when you were near the ocean. You come back at night only to discover that someone has programmed the TV radio with ocean sounds! That would be rather wow, would it not!

Breakfast

Breakfast in a hotel can be a wonderful experience. For a start, you don't have to cook it yourself :-), but you are of course at the same time paying for it so hopefully it's going to be good. For the breakfast product in a hotel to be good, two very basic things have to be right to start with: there should be sufficient variety and it should be tasty. Sufficient variety means that you should have healthy choices as well as pastries, cereals and good old bacon and eggs and there should also be a sufficient variety of fruit juices, teas and coffees to be had. Of course, all of this has to be tasty and "up to standard".

Let's imagine that the variety is there and that it's all of good quality and tasty. Let's do the same as we did for the bed and the sleeping experience. A few questions: What if you have complained that your coffee is cold and nothing is done about it? What if you have asked for some extra bread and you just don't get any? What if you have to wait in an absolutely massive queue in order to get to the breakfast buffet?

In spite of the fact that that the food is good and tasty once you manage to get it, you will have waited a long time to get there and finished up with cold coffee and no bread! As an individual, would you then still qualify this as a great breakfast experience?

What if, on the other hand, your coffee was replaced with hot coffee, you got the bread as soon as you asked for it and, on top of that, the employee that did these things did it proficiently and with a smile. You'd be happier, then, about your overall experience wouldn't you?

In addition, imagine that there was indeed a queue at breakfast but that whilst you were waiting an employee came to speak to you both apologising about the waiting time and telling you just how long you would have to wait. Even better, imagine that the employee at reception when you arrived at the hotel told you when was the best time to go to breakfast in order to avoid queuing? If all of these things happened, I think you would agree that the overall breakfast experience would be even better.

Broadband

You are still in the hotel and have had a great night's sleep and a fantastic breakfast experience and now you want to either check your mails or stream your favourite film on your computer.

But "lo and behold", you have no internet connection; Wi-Fi is not working. You are not going to be happy, particularly if you are in a hurry to check your mails for work. So you phone reception and ask if this can be fixed only to be told, "This often happens in the rooms on the third floor; you're probably best to go to the Internet café which is a mile from the hotel". So not only does it not work but you've just been told to go and spend your "hard earned" cash for a service outside the hotel which should be offered by the hotel for free.

Do you think that you are going to be happy about this? Probably not, I would think. But what if the employee at the reception had first of all apologised for the inconvenience, telling you that the IT department had not yet found out what was up with the system today but would be "on it" till it was fixed. She then goes on to tell you that the Wi-Fi is functioning in the lounge bar area of the hotel and that the hotel would be happy to offer you a free beverage whilst you are using this service to make up for any inconvenience caused. I hope you agree that this is a much better solution.

Of course, it still would be much better in the long run if the Wi-Fi is not only working perfectly all of the time, but that, in addition, the broadband is sufficient to allow as many people to use it at the same time without interference or the Wi-Fi slowing down (even if there are a few of us streaming our favourite films).

Good Wi-Fi connection in a hotel today is no longer an option, it is an absolute necessity.

Bath

Having a bath or, more commonly, a shower is for the vast majority of us extremely important. As with the sleeping experience, we can also talk about the "bathing or shower experience" in a hotel.

If you have a had a long hard day at work or have spent a long day walking around a city taking in all the "sites" on a hot day in summer, you will very probably be looking forward to both a relaxing and refreshing bathing experience. So when you get back to the hotel and the shower is not working at all or there is no hot water ("une douche à l'écossaise" is not always a source of pleasure for all), you are probably going to be disappointed at the very least.

If, added to that, the shower cannot immediately be repaired or none of the employees can offer you an alternative solution, you might eventually become angry and this would then probably end up being a good reason not to stay with this hotel (or hotel chain) ever again.

Now, instead of going through what the employees could have hypothetically done to alleviate this situation or simply solve the problem, I would like to share a personal experience which happened to me very recently in a hotel.

I went to take my shower and discovered that the water was not going to the shower head and that there was no way to divert it there. I was rather tired on that particular day and so I thought to myself "why not take a bath for once, it might be nice and relaxing and it might make a nice change from taking a shower?" So you can imagine that I was then a bit "miffed" when I discovered that there was no bath plug and that plan B was not going to happen☹.

Did I phone reception? No, as I said, I was rather tired and it was late. So I decided to wash up in the bath like in the "good old days" and in actual fact it wasn't so bad (but please don't try and imagine the scene!). Nevertheless, I had firmly decided that evening to give the reception "a piece of my mind" the following morning.

When I got to reception the next morning and finished explaining myself, not only did the employee apologise profusely but assured me that this would be fixed during the day and, furthermore, asked if they could do anything further to ensure that the rest of my stay would be as comfortable as possible. I was satisfied with this approach by the employee and will let you imagine what might have happened had the shower not been fixed and there had been no apology.

The point here is that a lot of things can go wrong with a bathing experience in a hotel (no hot or cold water, the temperature going up and down too much when you are in the shower, the bath being dirty and the list goes on . . .). So, if you already have a bathing experience which is not up to scratch for whatever the reason, you can only depend on the employees to sort it out.

Getting away for a minute from the hotel industry, we are all clients, customers or consumers during our day-to-day lives and all of us have a lot to be getting on with. We all remember that person who was particularly rude to us at the train station when we asked for some information or the employee at the till who did not smile at us, asked us to pay and then, to add insult to injury, asked to look into our bag to ensure that we had not stolen anything.

Or, what about when you are in the restaurant and you have been there for at least half an hour and no one has offered either yourself or your family a drink, whilst at the same time the two families that arrived well after you are already digging into their main course?
To finish off, you go to the hairdresser the next day and end up with a haircut making you look like you are going to

join the army (this is not what you asked for but the employee was too busy talking to her colleagues to listen to you).

So, in our day-to-day lives, we can all have bad experiences or frustrations related to how we are treated by employees in a lot of different areas of our lives. The good news is that we can also have fantastic experiences related to the behaviour of employees and how we interact with them. For example, I did personally get a very bad haircut recently and whilst I had some spare time walked into another hairdresser who had nothing to do with this and asked if they could fix it. Not only did the employee fix it in about five minutes flat, but when I asked what I owed for this, he said "oh nothing, just glad to be able to help". I can share with you that I will now become a permanent client of this salon in spite of the fact that it is really not close to where I live and that it might be quite a bit more expensive than the others.

One last personal experience (I promise!). Anyone who knows me knows that I am a fanatical fisherman. You've all heard about golfing widows, right, so how about a bit of sympathy for all those fishing widows out there? I digress, the story goes as follows. I have recently taken up fishing from the beach and had spent quite a fair amount of money buying all the necessary equipment (rods and reels, etc.).

During one of my first fishing trips with the new gear, I discovered that one of the reels was not working properly and this ruined my day out a little bit. Before I even got to the fishing tackle shop, I thought "I bet they're going to tell me that the equipment is fine, I just don't know how to use it or, even worse, they are going to tell me that it's me that broke the equipment and that the guarantee won't cover it".

I had in fact gone through a large number of scenarios before I even got there, the vast majority of which had negative outcomes for both me and my credit card.

So, imagine my relief when none of these scenarios happened. Instead, when I arrived, the employee who had sold me the equipment came to see me and check if everything was fine with the equipment sold. When I told him there was a problem with one of the reels, he immediately told me that he would replace this faulty equipment at no charge as well as test it so as to ensure that I would not have the same problem or inconvenience! Needless to say, I am now an extremely loyal client of this shop.

All of the examples that I have used have one thing in common. That is to say that even when the basic service or product is not up to standard, employees and the service that they provide (or not in certain cases) will make the difference as to whether the customer perception of the overall product offering will be good or bad.

As a case in point, when you are deciding where to go on vacation this year or choosing the hotel or accommodation for your stay, like most people you are probably going to do some research in this regard.
Potential customers/clients are today using more and more sites such as Trip Advisor or other "review sites" to help them decide what to choose and where to go. Bad reviews on these sites can have disastrous results for the

companies involved as I said earlier in the book (lowering the number of reservations and hence profits).

If you take the time to look at both the negative and positive comments on Trip Advisor, you might come to the same conclusion as I have (and I have looked at an awful lot of these during the course of my career).

The thing that is mentioned the most by far for both negative and positive comments is the service within hotels and not the product! This is not to say that the product is never mentioned, it is, but what really puts Trip Advisor scores up or down is people and the way that they interact and behave with your customers.

This brings us once again to the same conclusion as before: *employees really are the most important asset that a company has.* If you look at the negative examples from just a little earlier, you can see that if the employees at fault had had proper training, been empowered so as to take initiatives and happy, most, if not all, of these situations would have been easily resolved.

The bottom line really is that you can have a fantastic product but that without great employees you might find that however "wow" your product is, it might just remain only that, a product sitting on the shelf.

In summary:

I would choose fantastic employees over a fantastic product every time.

Conclusion

Conclusion

I think we can all agree that in order to be successful in any business venture, we need to make the best use of our internal resources in order to produce a product or service that clients will buy and keep buying.

The resources that we should normally have in some shape or form can be put into or under the heading of four main categories: physical (such as buildings or machines), financial (capital), intellectual property (copyright, brand, patents) and, last but not least, human (your employees).

Let's pretend that you are in the hotel business and that you have a beautiful building with fantastic fixtures and fittings (so you have the financial resources) and you think that you have a good brand (whether you are five stars, a boutique hotel or more of an economy hotel).

All of this sounds great as long as you remember that the mere fact that you have a brand which can be recognised by customers or potential customers means that somewhere along the way you have made a **customer promise**.

Your customer promise might be "you will feel welcome here" or "a home from home" or "the ultimate in five star luxury".

Let's further hypothesise by saying that it is the last of these and that you have, once again, a fabulous looking hotel with all the facilities and services imaginable. That may be true, but IF the employees that are running the hotel are not delivering the service correctly, you are going to have a major problem due to the fact that the service will be in complete contrast as compared with your product.

In actual fact, in this case, you would probably be better off with a product not quite up to scratch but with fantastic customer service delivered by your employees. If we take this reasoning further, we could say:

"Better to have a poor product and great staff than a great product and poor staff."

This is because, in the first case, you will have surprise (even to the point of delighting certain clients), whereas, in the second case, you are setting your clients up to be disappointed!

What I am underlining once again is that the primary resource for your company is your employees. Without employees who are properly trained, who are allowed to participate actively in the life of the organisation and who are happy to be at work (through being recognised for what they do), you don't have much chance of keeping your guests or clients happy or indeed of keeping them or making them loyal customers at all!

Yet another way of looking at this in the case of hotels is to look at what the main key success factors for hotels are. From my experience, the four key factors are:

➢ Differentiation of the product.
➢ Quality of service.
➢ How to adapt to the economy (adaptability).
➢ Pricing strategy.

Addressing each of these points in turn, the main type of differentiation possible in a service industry is the type or level of service itself, which is what inevitably leads to quality of service. In order to be adaptable to change (economic, technological, political, etc.), your employees need to be agile and they are not likely to be agile unless they have been properly treated and empowered.

As for the last point, you are not going to be able to charge premium prices unless the service levels can justify this. The only people who are going to make this happen are your employees.

What I have attempted to do in this book is to show why it is that employees are the most important resource for any company or organisation and how to go about ensuring that they engage with the company.

From my experience, what has been talked about in this book works but it also requires a good deal of endeavour. Then, again, if everything really worthwhile was free and without investment, I'm sure that someone would have found out by now.

Thank you for having taken the time to read this book and thank you on behalf of your employees, both now and in the future, for putting it into practice.